ALL NIGHT LONG

ALL NIGHT LONG

How to Make Love to a Man Over 50

BARBARA KEESLING, PH.D.

▣   ▣   ▣

HarperCollins*Publishers*

HarperCollins books may be purchased for educational, business, or sales promotional use. For information please write: Special Markets Department, HarperCollins Publishers Inc., 10 East 53rd Street, New York, NY 10022.

FIRST EDITION

Designed by Interrobang Design Studio

Printed on acid-free paper

Library of Congress Cataloging-in-Publication Data
Keesling, Barbara.
    All night long : how to make love to a man over 50 / Barbara Keesling.
        p. cm.
    Includes index.
    ISBN 0-06-019302-6
    1. Sex instruction for women. 2. Middle aged men—Sexual behavior. 3. Aged men—Sexual behavior. 4. Aging—Psychological aspects. 5. Sexual disorders. 6. Sexual exercises. I. Title.
HQ46.K42 2000
613.9'6—DC21   99-086106

00 01 02 03 04 ❖/RRD 10 9 8 7 6 5 4 3 2 1

Contents

Introduction

The man you love is turning fifty. How will this affect his desire? How will this affect his ability to perform? How will this affect your relationship? Is there still great sex in your future? If you care about your partner, I know you want answers to these questions. *Every* woman wants answers to these questions, and they are answers you deserve to have.

Doctors tell us that if a man is in good physical health, there is no medical reason for his sexual performance to change. Not if he is 50. Or 60. Or 70. Or even older. Yet things *do* change. And as partners, we see these changes.

- We see changes in our partner's desire and changes in his drive.
- We see changes in his erections and in the intensity of his ejaculations.
- We see changes in his "staying power" and in his overall strength.
- We see changes in his self-image and changes in his confidence.

We see all kinds of changes, some small and some not so small. We watch our partner try to adapt to these changes; we watch ourselves try to adapt to these changes. And we wonder what will be changing next.

I am a sex therapist who has been in private practice for more than ten years. I have written many books about important sexual issues, but this issue is nearest and dearest to my heart. I also have a radio show in southern California, and this is one issue that is guaranteed to trigger a lively conversation. On my radio show, there is something I tell my listeners at every opportunity—it is a personal mantra that I want them to embrace. In my practice as a sex therapist, I offer the very same mantra to all of my clients. And now I'm going to offer it to you:

Love Begins at 50, and Lust Begins at 50

How can I say this with such confidence? Because as a sex therapist—and before that, a sexual surrogate—I have worked with *hundreds* of men in their fifties, sixties, seventies and even eighties, and I see their real potential every day. I see them grow and evolve; I see them become more loving, caring, sensual and outright sexual. Often, I see complete sexual transformations. And, I must add, I have also been fortunate enough to witness this in my personal life.

What I'm trying to say here is that I know from extensive experience—both personal and professional—

that *turning 50 can be one of the most powerful and positive sexual passages in a man's life,* and I know that it can have a magical effect on a loving relationship. Yet I also know that you don't have my experience. I know that you probably have only *one* man in your life, and you don't know *what* to expect. How could you? And this is why it has been so important for me to be able to write this book. I want you to learn what I have learned, to know what I know. I want you to be able to look forward to your sexual future with confidence and excitement and anticipation. With the right information and the right tools, there is no reason you cannot.

Turning 50 is scary for *everyone.* But it is particularly scary for any man who fears he could lose his potency. There are so many negative myths and negative attitudes in our culture that feed into this fear. The word *impotence* is tossed around as though it is a prescription for every man's future that cannot be escaped. Yet the fact is that male sexual functioning is completely misunderstood by most men *and* women, including the "experts." And "impotence" is usually not impotence at all, but a combination of simple factors that have a powerful effect on a man's penis—factors such as stimulation, lubrication, stress and sleep—coupled with a loss of confidence.

This book is going to prove to you, once and for all, that getting older truly is getting better. I'm going to help you understand men's fears (penetration anxiety, "shrinkage," fear of failure, fear of being judged, etc.). I'm going to help you conquer destructive myths and shatter bad attitudes you may be holding on to. And I'm going to teach you exercises that give both you and your partner a sense of strength, vitality, pleasure and control that will result in the best sex ever.

Forget what you have been told in the past. Sex is *great* at 50, and beyond. If your experience has been different, that is about to change. And it will change by the time you have finished this book.

Love Begins at 50
(And You Don't Need a Pill!)

This is not a book about Viagra. I need to make that clear before we get started because I know it's on your mind; these days, it's on *everybody's* minds. In the next ten chapters I am going to share a comprehensive sexual anti-aging formula that I developed over the past ten years with my colleagues—sex therapists, urologists, psychologists and cardiologists—and my wonderful clients. But there isn't any little blue pill called Viagra in this potent formula. And if you think I'm going to spend most of this book talking about "magic pills" such as Viagra, you don't know me very well. **My anti-aging formula isn't something you can buy with a prescription, or purchase over the counter** (though you might discover some of it under the table!). It does not come in pill form. It is a program of simple exercises that anyone can learn, combined with basic wisdom that every man and woman can embrace. And the only one who is qualified to dispense it is *you*.

I first decided to write this book before the introduction of Viagra. Then this "magic pill" appeared, followed by copycats, wannabes, herbal alternatives and new, improved versions. For a while, it seemed as though the universe had been turned on its ear as millions of prescriptions were being handed out around the globe and pharmacists were suddenly busier than they could ever remember. It looked as though sex after 50 would be something we would get in a pill. "Take two, and call me when you're ready." Would that become our rallying cry? For a while, everyone wondered. Even I wondered. For a while.

We all know what pills such as Viagra *can* do— they can help many men get an effective erection.* But it took a little longer for most of us to discover what Viagra, and other magic little pills, *can't* do. It also took a little longer for us to discover that for the vast majority of men over 50—men who are not clinically impotent—these pills can actually interfere with healthy, natural, incredibly positive sensual and sexual changes that time provides free of charge.

---

*PLEASE NOTE: *EVERY* man should consult his physician and carefully evaluate his personal risks before ever taking any of these medicines. Contraindications are serious and often life-threatening.

I have no interest in passing judgment on any performance-enhancing medication (particularly medications that are endorsed by distinguished former members of Congress!). I'm glad men have such medicines and remedies available to them. I'm all for anything that gives more people the opportunity to enjoy sex, and it's important to have options. But I think it is more important to point out the limitations of *any* solution—be it this year's medical miracle, next year's and so forth—that comes in pill form. And we need to start with the biggest limitation of all: A pill may give a man an erection, but it doesn't necessarily make him more sensual, more caring or more loving. To the contrary, it can actually *decrease* his motivation to become a better partner, particularly if he's a man who equates having an erection with being a satisfying lover.

I call this "erection-first thinking." "I've got an erection," he tells himself, "what else do you need?" And that is the end of sexual growth. Perhaps this limitation is not obvious to you, but it is obvious to a professional sex therapist whose goal is increased intimacy and gratification. Maybe you have been doing a little "erection-first thinking" of your own.

The focus has to be on lovemaking, not erections— on *partnership*, not performance. Yes, we want our partner to have an erection! For his enjoyment, and for ours. But what we want more than anything is to have a partner we can *make love to*. It is our heart

and soul that we want to have penetrated. We want
this kind of penetration when our partner is 50, and
60, and 70, and 80. An erection can't do that. A pill
can't do that. Only making love to the man we love
can do that.

Sharing Secrets: *You* Are the Most Special Ingredient in This Anti-Aging Formula

So if there is no medicine in my secret formula, what
is this fountain of sexual youth? I will share everything with you in the pages that follow. I will share all
of my secrets, even the ones I hold most dear. But you
need to know right now that the key ingredient in this
erotic recipe is *you*. *Your* interest. *Your* attitude. *Your*
support. *Your* openness. *Your* enthusiasm. *Your* willingness to experiment. *Your* love. And your willingness to work: your willingness to work with your
partner to have the kind of sex life you want.

This book is for *you*. Much of it you will choose to
share with the man you love. Perhaps you will
encourage him to read it from cover to cover. But it is
for you, because you are the catalyst for change.

By following a program of simple exercises, learning a few easy-to-master sexual techniques and
acquiring some basic information that will foster an
open, loving attitude, you can keep your man—and
yourself—sexually fit, sexually focused and sexually
fabulous for decades. It doesn't require any pills or
gadgets. It doesn't require a Ph.D. The only require-

ment is the love between you and your partner, and a shared desire to keep your sex life special. If you have that, the rest is easy. You just need to get started.

From my professional and personal experience I know that most women want to do the right thing for their partners. And the fact that you are reading this book right now only proves my point. I know that you want to be helpful and that you want to be understanding. And I know that your love is strong. But I also know that you want to continue to have a sex life that is gratifying, if not downright thrilling. And guess what? That's not a selfish thing. You *should* have a great sex life for years to come. And you can! It doesn't take a miracle. You simply need to know how to make love to a man over 50!

Until Now, He's Probably Had It Easy

Women have been conditioned to experience their sexuality as a complex fabric of desire, mood, tension, timing and chemistry. Part of this is physiological and part of this is cultural, but it's all a part of who we are. Most of the time we love the richness of our sexuality, and it is hard to imagine it being any other way, but we also know that it can be a lot of work. A *lot* of work.

How different it can be for men! Though we may not want to trade places, we can certainly be envious of men's sexuality at times, or even awestruck on occasion. Mind you, I'm not talking penis envy here,

I'm talking about simple envy for a style of sexuality that seems so much less complex: Man sees woman. Man gets excited by seeing woman. Man gets even more excited by touching woman. Man is ready to have sex with woman. Wow. For a lot of lucky men, it does not get a lot more complex for many years of their adult life. The equipment may not be perfect, but it works well enough to get the job done, and that's good enough for him.

Of course man wants to please woman (we hope), and this may create some anxiety. And man may not have a lot of "staying power," which can also create some anxiety and feelings of inadequacy. And man may feel that his performance and "equipment" are being judged by woman (even if *he* is really the one who is doing all the judging), which may also create some anxiety. And every man has his good and bad days. But unless man is prone to having erection problems, the hardest part of sex—i.e., the turn-on— does not require tons of work. And the efficiency of the male hydraulic system makes it all too easy for many men to avoid the harder work of becoming more connected, attentive lovers.

I do not want to support obvious stereotypes, or paint a picture with too broad a brush. There are certainly many very sensitive, sophisticated male lovers under the age of 50 who are very connected to their sexuality. There are many who work very hard in bed (a few who work *too* hard), and there are many who worry. But most men do not *have* to learn how to be sophisticated lovers as long as there is a little "gas in the engine." In many ways, they *do* have it very easy, certainly easy compared to women. Until, that is, they start turning 50.

The Best News About Turning 50

After 50, something very powerful happens: Men begin to slow down. Sexual interest is less consistent and also less predictable, and interest doesn't necessarily guarantee "results" (i.e., instantaneous physical arousal). Erections are a little less perfect, or even a lot less perfect. Arousal becomes more labor-intensive—more in need of "hands-on" support. Orgasms diminish in their intensity, and may also require more work to achieve—more stimulation or more forceful stimulation or more specific stimulation. Even ejaculation can become less powerful and plentiful, leading to a different experience of "release." These are *normal, natural* **physiological** changes that have nothing to do with the quality of your relationship or the cut of your negligee. It's part of being human and being a man.

Maybe these changes aren't noticeable or significant until the age of 55 or 60. Or, for a few lucky (or perhaps not so lucky—I'll let you decide) men, until the age of 70 or even 80. But sooner or later, things start to change. Not surprisingly, these changes are not welcome. Issues of virility and potency are immediately questioned. New anxieties (such as "penetration anxiety") surface. The issue of mortality rears its sobering head. The days of worry-free sex seem to be over. This kind of sexual change can leave a man quite shaken. And it can also rattle the woman he loves.

Yet this seemingly bad news is actually the best news—news that calls for celebration. How can I say this? Because, sexually speaking, slowing down is truly a *wonderful* thing, wonderful because it is an education. And more wonderful because it is a genuine *opportunity* for sexual growth and change. Of course, it may be a bit unsettling at first. And your partner's first instinct may be to start closing sexual doors. But if you are ready and willing to help him keep those doors open, it is a change of life that is packed with potential.

The man you love is actually slowing down enough to "come into" his body. He is actually feeling subtleties in his own sexuality and sensuality, perhaps for the first time. He's going to start noticing. He's going to start caring. And yes, he may start worrying, too. But all of these changes are going to make him more motivated to learn and try new things.

When you add it all together, what this really means is that **this is your partner's big chance—his big chance to become more caring, more tuned in, more open, more vulnerable and even more loving**. All of this is possible if the transition is handled well. And that is where *you* will make all of the difference.

But it isn't just about *him*. This is also your big chance as a *couple*. As a couple, this is your entree into a more loving, more intimate, more intensely sexual bond. It is your chance to learn together, confront change together and grow together. In the words of Alexandra Penney, bestselling author of *How to Make Love to a Man*: "Once you realize that men aren't perfectly tuned sex machines—they're lovably human—and you become sensitive to their special problems, you've taken a giant step toward breaking down barriers that stand in the way of love and intimacy." And, I would like to add, it's never too late to get started.

The Opportunity of a Lifetime

I keep using the word "opportunity," and I'm about to use it some more. Think about it: For the first time in a very long time (perhaps the first time ever), the man you love has a reason to pay closer attention to his sexuality *and* to your sexuality. This is a real *opportunity* for him to learn about the complexities of his physiology and the intricacies of his arousal—a process that will naturally attune him more to *your* body and *your* needs. It is an *opportunity* for both of you to go off automatic pilot and start to explore. It is an *opportunity* for his lovemaking to become more comprehensive, more enlightened and more fulfilling for both of you! This is the stuff of great beginnings. It is what you have really been waiting for, hoping for and perhaps even asking for. It is the powerful and positive change that "magic" pills just mess up. And it enters naturally into your relationship as a gift from Father Time.

Yes, it's scary. Change is always scary. But here's the bottom line: The good stuff is about to *begin* if you will just open that door. The man you love may be getting older, but your sex is about to get better. *Much* better. And it will all unfold under the direction of your loving, caring hand. The key is how the various changes are handled. And that is what this book is really about: how to handle his changes in the service of your mutual pleasure. Not how to *accommodate* his changes. Not how to *settle* for less or survive with less. But how to work with his changes—and *your* changes, too—to bring out a more loving, more responsive, more vital, more sexual partner who will keep you engaged and feeling loved for decades to come.

So the first thing you must do is relax and take a few deep breaths. Give your partner a loving hug (you don't need to tell him why!). Now prepare to take your sexual relationship off automatic pilot and take control of the wheel.

Your Challenge: Going Off Automatic Pilot

Whatever it is you have been doing with your partner, sexually speaking, you've probably been doing it for a very long time. Perhaps in the first few years of your relationship there was considerable experimentation as you worked your way through the sexual learning curve. Perhaps there were moments of confusion, miscommunication, even frustration. Maybe you didn't get everything you dreamed of; maybe your partner made some sacrifices, too. But over time you both figured out ways to give enough and get enough. You became content, and your sexual relationship kicked over to automatic pilot—a comforting cruise control.

Most couples develop comfortable sexual routines that carry them through years and years of their relationship, hoping that nothing will ever rock the boat too forcefully, or for any length of time. Sure, once in a while you might surprise your partner with a new pair of sexy panties or a steamy video. And there may be the occasional disruption due to illness or other extenuating circumstances. But it is your routine that you always return to; this is the thing you trust, and you trust your partner's ability to participate with predictability.

Some women will be able to count on this predictability for the lifetime of their relationship. There may be small changes, but nothing that demands your attention or a break in the routine. I know these women consider themselves fortunate. I feel somewhat different. I consider any opportunity for sexual growth to be fortunate. I consider any opportunity for sexual experimentation fortunate. I consider any opportunity for sexual reeducation fortunate. And I'm going to tell you why.

In my opinion, sexual intimacy is the Holy Grail. There is no place where we can be as vulnerable, as open, as responsive, as free and as connected to both our partner and ourselves. Your sexual routine may be very gratifying, but it is not necessarily freeing. You may trust it and enjoy it, but it probably doesn't give you the shivers. But now, if you are *lucky*, having your partner turn 50 brings a break in the routine. And while this break in the routine requires your attention, and a little bit of work, it also has the potential to translate into something hot . . . white-hot.

You are making love to someone new. Someone you have known, perhaps, forever, but must get to know all over again. This is a time for experimentation. And experimentation is exciting. You're going to be trying new things, and that is exciting. You're going to be taking chances, and that is exciting. You're going to be thinking about sex a lot more, and that's exciting. You might even be talking about sex more—that's exciting, too. Maybe you have always had a small case of "sex on the brain," but now it's going to be front and center. That is going to heat you up. And it's going to make things nice and toasty for your partner, too.

Sure, someday you might return to automatic status. But today is not that day. Today you are starting a very different journey. And your job is to enjoy the ride.

Most Men Have Spent Years Learning How
Not to Feel

It is a basic fact of male sexuality that most men spend half of their sexual lives trying not to feel. That's right, trying *not* to feel. I need to explain this to you very carefully so that you have a crystal-clear picture of the male experience prior to age 50.

The day that giving a woman pleasure became an important goal for most men was both the best and worst day of their sexual lives. On the one hand, there was finally a true appreciation of female sexuality, female desire and female need. This was a milestone for men, and truly fabulous for us! On the other hand, all of this appreciation and concern translated into one concrete, practical challenge for men: trying to last longer to please the woman. Fabulous, once again, for us, but not so fabulous for them. A great idea in theory, but not in the execution. Why? Because, as most men quickly discovered, prolonging intercourse is a lot more difficult than it sounds.

Trying to last longer has been a double-edged sword for men since it became a goal. This is because for most men, trying to prolong intercourse and delay orgasm has become a lifelong exercise in trying *not* to feel.

Consider how long it takes the average young man to masturbate himself to orgasm. One minute. Two minutes. Three minutes if he really wants to turn it into a big production. (Some men brag that they can get off in 30 seconds!) Now imagine this very same man trying to have intercourse with his partner for five minutes or ten minutes or twenty minutes or an hour! How is that going to be possible? For most men, the answer is very simple: Train yourself to *not* feel.

Prolonging intercourse through *de*sensitization is an obsession for most men that begins in the teenage years and carries through in perpetuity. Men invest countless dollars in condoms and special creams because these things desensitize the penis, allowing a man to last longer by feeling *less*. "Look at the ceiling." "Look at the floor." "Just don't look at her!" "Pretend you're at a baseball game." "Pretend you're at a funeral." "Pretend you're with your grandmother." This is some of the advice men offer each other in locker-room conversation. And these primitive techniques are popular among men seeking a quick and effective solution because as silly as the techniques may seem, they change the focus, detract from a man's sensations and his excitement and enable him to last longer by feeling *less*.

For most men, the search for sexual advice begins in the teenage years, when there is the first experience of sexual consciousness outside the "me." By the time a man is in his twenties, he has found some viable solution, however awkward. And as the years accumulate, it becomes a fixture of his sexual personality.

One very honest client of mine explained how this

impacted on his sexual development: "As a young guy, I was always a 'quick gun'—one minute of screwing seemed like an eternity. My very first girlfriends didn't seem to mind. If they did, they certainly never said anything. But as I got older, that shifted, and it became very clear to me that sixty seconds of intercourse was barely long enough to get a woman's attention. This was a real problem for me. I was embarrassed to ask anyone about this, and was always straining to overhear other guys talking about this very same challenge. At some point I remember reading an article or story—probably in *Playboy* magazine—about men who could distract themselves by thinking about the weather, or the news, or the ball scores. I tried, and it helped. Then I started experimenting with other ways to distract myself. I would look around the room, but this would make some women angry. Then I started fantasizing that I was making love to someone *less* attractive. That worked, except that occasionally it worked too well and I would lose my hard-on."

This client's story is not atypical. Almost every man has found some kind of gimmick that enables him to last longer by feeling *less*. For most men, including this client of mine, the most effective gimmick is to keep one's attention far away from one's own pleasure and from the physical and emotional sources of that pleasure. These techniques may be very effective for an 18-year-old, or a 25-year-old, or even a 40-year-old. But as a man continues to age, and the penis ceases to be the perfect soldier, these techniques begin to create more problems than they solve.

This is *exactly* the physical and psychological place where men have to start their *unlearning* as they turn 50 and the body starts to slow down. **The sexual agenda and sexual solutions of an 18-year-old do not fit on the frame of a man in his fifties, sixties or seventies**—not in spirit and not in design. The days of buying into his adolescent agenda are over. If your partner is to feel his power as a lover, that ancient agenda needs to be rewritten. And the only way that will happen is through a new experience of his *and* your excitement.

His Challenge: Learning to Feel *More* Sexual

So you can see that the man you love has his own version of automatic pilot that he must disengage from. His sexual routine has to change. His sexual mindset has to change. And he must learn to feel *more* sexual. He needs to go back to sexual boot camp. And he needs to know that you are right there with him.

With your help, your partner is going to unlearn all of his old habits, his distancing techniques and desensitization techniques, and experience the full weight of his sexuality for the first time. Instead of running away from his own sensations, he is going to turn around and face them head on. He is going to meet his penis. He is going to learn about excitement. He is going to embrace his own arousal. He is going to release himself into his own orgasm. He is going to learn how to get lost in his own body, and how to get lost in your body. No more baseball fantasies and nasty images of Grandma. The man you love is about to discover everything he has been missing—one small step at a time. And it is you who will be leading the way.

This is going to be new, and it is going to be different, but it will never be intimidating or overwhelming because it is going to happen SLOWLY and INCREMENTALLY.

Many times, your partner won't even realize you are introducing something new or different into your lovemaking. He won't notice because it's going to be so natural—perhaps more natural than anything he has ever experienced sexually. Remember that all of his life, your partner has been working *against* his most powerful sexual self. Now you are bringing him into alignment. You are helping him discover the sleeping giant that has been there all along, helping him make connections he had to sever, find impulses he had to censor and experience sensations he had to repress or ignore. Don't be surprised if this makes him forget he has turned 50, because he will be feeling the sexual confidence and vigor of a very young man!

The Proactive Solution: Creating Something Wonderful

Change is always intimidating, even when it is clear that it is something very positive. Right now, you are poised at the threshold to a new beginning. The question is: Are you ready to cross that threshold and enter a new world?

When it comes to sex, I make no judgments about other people's choices. If you are comfortable with the status quo in your sexual relationship, I don't have a problem with that. You shouldn't, either. If you want to adopt a wait-and-see attitude, I don't have a problem with that. You shouldn't, either. Sex doesn't have to be perfect to be fulfilling. I'm going to say that again. **Sex doesn't have to be perfect to be fulfilling.** Love goes a long way to fill in some of those spaces.

Having said that, however, let me now say this: Speaking both professionally and personally, I have a very proactive approach to sex and aging. I can sum up *my* attitude in just three words: "Get started now." My goal is always to make sexual transitions so seamless that no one has to think or feel there was ever a problem. Being proactive eliminates the bad bumps; I think this is the kindest gift you can give to both yourself and the man you love.

By putting the information in this book to work for you now, you will always be able to stay at least one step ahead of the age curve. You will always be months or even years ahead of potential transitions, neutralizing their potential fallout. What a relief that will be for both of you! Recognize also that whether or not your partner is beginning to show his age, there is always *something* that can make your sexual connection more gratifying. *Everything* you do makes a difference—especially if you start working now to create a new sexual foundation that will hold up to the forces of Father Time.

I don't expect you to be just like me. But I think it is important that you are able to make informed decisions. That is why my goal is to give you *all* of the information, exercises and techniques you will ever need *right now*. With this information, these exercises and these techniques, you can make informed decisions—you can make them now, three months from now, three years from now and thirty years from now. The truth is, the moment you have all of this new material at your fingertips, you will already be changing —changing internally. These internal changes have a way of entering into your sexual relationship without any effort or conscious intention. New information creates new attitudes, and new attitudes create new behavior. It's a more subtle kind of change—change by osmosis—but it is significant. This is your first small reward for being open and interested.

The important thing to recognize is that you have many choices here. As the person who has the book in her hand, you are in control. You can read everything I have to offer, and then choose to watch and wait.

That is certainly a valid choice. You can read everything I have to offer, then pick and choose what you
might like to try. Another valid choice. You can follow *all* of my suggestions and master all the possibilities. That's wonderful. But you need to know I don't
expect that or ask for that. While it is my job to tell
you everything I can that might be helpful or useful, it
is your job to decide what feels best for you and your
partner in your situation right now. That is part of
what it means to be a caring partner. If you read
through this book, I will have accomplished my goal.
If you read through this book, I am sure that whatever you choose—now, ten years from now or twenty
years from now—you will be choosing what is best
for you and your partner. I want you to have this
information. I need you to know you have options. By
the time you have finished reading this book, you *will*
know. And the moment you start experimenting with
your first new exercise or technique, you will *feel*
those options. The rest is up to you.

How to Talk (or Not Talk) to Your Partner About This Book

The moment you picked up this book, you *started*
talking to your partner about your sexual relationship. I'm talking about the quiet conversations you
began having in your own mind, imagining (and
rehearsing) what it would be like to actually have
them out loud. Looking at this book is also a shift in

your behavior. That shift has a way of "talking" to your partner, too, even though the conversations are nonverbal. Your body language is changing; your sexual energy is changing; your sexual intent is changing. Your partner may not see or understand these changes, but he is already *feeling* these changes. It happens that fast.

But the question arises: How much talking—real, out-loud conversation—is appropriate here? As I hinted before, that depends very much on you, your partner and your relationship. Only you can judge. But think about your partner *first*.

Some men are very open to all new things of a sexual nature. If your partner is one such man, you may choose to read this book together, or give him his own copy to dog-ear. Even the simple act of having a shared read is sometimes enough to jump-start a man right out of his post–50 doldrums because it makes it crystal clear that regardless of what *he* is going through, you are still excited at the thought of having sex with him. **A lot of men start to shut down after 50 in nervous anticipation of their partner shutting down.** If you are giving a different message—one that says, "Hey, Mister, I don't care whether or not you're slowing down, we're just getting started!"—you will help your partner avoid that common after-50 pitfall. The title of this book gives this message. It says to your partner, "I'm not thinking about Brad Pitt or those guys who model underwear—it's *you* I'm think-

ing about. *You* are my sexual fantasy. *You* are the guy
who gets me hot."

At the other end of the continuum, there are, of
course, some men who experience any sex book as a
demand or a judgment. For these men, the introduction of a new book—*any* new book—implies that
things are not okay the way they are. If your partner
is sensitive in this way, sharing the book right away is
probably not a good idea. Remember that open-
minded or not open-minded, your partner *is* going to
be very sensitive about the potential sexual ramifica-
tions of his age. If leaving this book on the nightstand
is going to add to his emotional load, what's the
point? Your partner does not need to read a single
page of this book to benefit from the majority of its
contents. The book has been written for *you*, not *him*.
As you *slooooowwwlllllyyyy* introduce the material in
this book into your sexual relationship—changes that
imbue your partner with strength and confidence and
sexual vitality—he will become more open to talking
and reading about the experience. Let that day arrive
on its own.

Regardless of your partner's eagerness and/or sensitivity and/or fearfulness, the very best advice I can
offer you is to *take your time*. This is not a contest. It
has taken at least 50 years for the man you love to
become the sexual person he is right now. You can't—
and shouldn't want to—overhaul that in five minutes.
Don't be like the interior decorator who comes into a

house and starts knocking down every wall and window, pulling up every carpet and pulling out every appliance in a flurry of frightening activity. **The idea is not to *scare* your partner into becoming the fabulous lover you know he can be—the idea is to facilitate a slow transformation that will endure.** You have the rest of your lives together to grow and explore. Start with something slow and simple: Just turn the page.

2

Shifting Gears

Change begins with the most subtle shift. And that shift has already occurred. You picked up this book—the first shift. You read the first chapter—another shift. Your mind, heart and body are opening to new possibilities—a huge shift. You are starting to fantasize about an exciting future. Yet another shift. And you haven't even completed a single exercise or learned a single new technique!

This is the way lasting change is supposed to begin: It is a slow groundswell that gains strength from its own sincere foundation. You are the cornerstone of that foundation, and that is how I know you will get the results you desire.

So where do we go from here? You actually have several choices. If you are feeling a little anxious right now about the sexual prognosis for a partner who has

passed his fiftieth birthday and you need the immediate comfort of hard information, I recommend that
you skip to chapters 3 and 5 for an overview of how,
when and why male sexuality changes after the age of
50. Then return to this chapter when you are done.
But if you are like most of my clients, you probably
want to get busy with some practical exercises that
you can introduce into your lovemaking right now.
This chapter has those exercises. This is the "hors
d'oeuvres" chapter—the finger food to soothe your
hunger until it is time for the big meal. There is nothing fancy here—nothing very clinical or complicated.
We'll be moving more in that direction later. The
exercises in *this* chapter are very simple and playful.
Think of them as gentle warm-up exercises like the
simple stretching you would do before starting a serious workout. They are the preparation—but preparation *is* important.

Some of the exercises in this chapter may seem so
simple you might be tempted to skip them. Others
may seem superfluous. And there may be some you
are already familiar with. Remember that I am giving
you *all* the tools I have in my professional arsenal; I
am leaving no stone unturned. You don't have to *try*
everything, but I would like you to *consider* everything. Each exercise is here for a reason, even if that
reason is only to get you thinking more about making
love.

Slowing Down to the Speed of Love

A client of mine, on her first visit to my office with her husband several months ago, pulled me aside at one point and said, "I have to be honest with you. I'm a very tired, very busy woman. What's the fastest possible way to light a fire under this man?" I paused, placed a hand on her shoulder, looked her straight in the eye and said, "Slow ... him ... down." It was not the answer she was looking for, and it was not the answer she expected, but it was the answer she needed. Her shoulders relaxed, her countenance changed and she became a different person in the room.

The title of this book is *not How to F—k a Man over 50*. And it is not *How to Get Your Guy to Get It Up ASAP*. This is a book about *making love*—making love to the man you love—and it will give you a lifetime of sexual pleasure if you let it in. Of course you are anxious and eager to implement change. But since you are the one who is going to be in charge here, you are the one who has to set the right pace, and **the sexual pace that gets results is SLOW.**

Speed kills. It kills romance. It kills sensuality, it kills sexual intensity. And it squeezes the life out of an orgasm. Yet most men under the age of 50 tend to live their sex life in the fastest lane. They like foreplay to be quick, they would *prefer* their intercourse to be intense, but not prolonged (even though they may *try* to prolong it to please a partner) and they don't seem interested in drawing out their own experience of orgasm. Quick, quick, quick. Ejaculate. Aahh . . . All in time for the eleven o'clock news.

This is not an indictment. It is simply the way many men are—a reality that you have probably experienced all too often with your partner. There are many reasons why a fast, furious pace is so satisfying for men—emotional reasons and physiological reasons. I have already touched on some of these reasons, and I will talk about this much more in later chapters. Whatever the reasons, you know the reality, and it is probably something you have learned to accept and accommodate.

But imagine what it would be like if making love were a celebration of SLOW. Imagine what it would feel like to be flirting again, to tease and be teased, to be romanced, to be sensually massaged and to make love without a stopwatch ticking. You are not going to have to imagine this much longer, because these are the kinds of changes that can happen as your partner slows down to the speed of love.

Don't get me wrong here. I still appreciate the value of an occasional quickie, and I know that some frantic screwing can be quite a thrill. But speed is not the thing that generates the most profound and consistent erotic intensity. Speed doesn't manufacture the real heat. That only comes from going SLOW.

Many women try for years to bring their partner's lovemaking to a less breakneck pace without killing his excitement and his interest. Yet this is a battle that very few women have won.

Guess what? That's going to change now, because your partner is changing. If anything, the man you love is starting to worry if he can keep up with *you*. He's not so sure he has the sexual intensity and staying power to keep pace with a woman who is still in her sexual prime. He is *ready* to slow down. He just needs to know that he *can*. And that's where you come in.

From this point forward, you need to lead your partner down the slower road. You need to show him through your actions, your reactions, your pleasure and your appreciation that slow is the way of the future. If he's starting to slow down naturally, you want to slow him down even *more*. Even if he hasn't started slowing down, you need to give him permission to change gears. You want to bring him to the speed that is sexiest for you—the speed that gives you the most pleasure. The time has arrived. From this point forward, slow but steady wins your heart.

Caution: Reckless Driver Ahead

There is one significant obstacle every woman will face as she tries to steer her partner down the road to SLOW, and I need to warn you now. It is the enemy of SLOW, and it is *his fear*.

As men age, and sense the body slowing down, their initial reaction is usually panic. Instead of feeling their way through the shift and accepting a different experience of arousal and erection, they try to turn up the juice. They start accelerating their movements and intensifying their touch. Everything becomes faster and firmer in an attempt to compensate for a slower, gentler experience of themselves. A man's playfulness contracts; foreplay becomes a luxury he's not sure he can afford. The moment he feels excited he may try to seize that moment by cutting to the chase (i.e., intercourse). Movements are rushed and more abrupt. His thrusting may intensify. Even when he is masturbating, he may try to force himself to quick orgasm instead of handling himself more gently. It's a primitive solution to his changing reality.

But as both you and your partner probably know from experience, his attempts to pick up speed are usually met with poor results *for both of you*. He is actually cutting himself off from his own full body experience; this guarantees he will feel *less*. In the process, he is also cutting *you* off from the full experience you need to get aroused. He may be able to have his orgasm, and you may get a few minutes of penetration, but everyone is left feeling a little bit cheated. Sometimes, a big bit.

Moving to the SLOW Lane

For you and your partner to make a glorious transition into life, love and lust after 50, you are going to have to give yourself, and your partner, permission to slow down. While it is important that this is reflected in your words, the most practical and powerful way to do this is with your actions. You should not be threatened by the fact that he is slowing down. You should be welcoming the changes, and celebrating the shift. Truth is, **your partner needs to slow down** **beyond** **the natural process of his body.** He needs to learn to crawl through intimate moments and feel everything—every nuance, every gesture, every impulse, every twinge. This is the only way for him to "come alive" and stay that way for decades. He *has* to learn how to feel, and you must lead the way. He is going to learn about his touch from your touch. He is going to learn about SLOW from your example.

From Today Forward, *Your* Organizing Theme Is SLOW

Starting today:

- Your kisses will be more deliberate and slow.
- Your gestures will be more deliberate and slow (the way, for example, you undress in his presence).
- Your caresses will be more deliberate and slow.
- When you massage him, it will be more deliberate and slow.
- When you use your hands or mouth to stimulate him, it will be more deliberate and slow.
- Every time your body rises up to meet the thrust of his penis, it will be more deliberate and slow.

I don't expect you to learn this overnight, and you don't have to. SLOW is a style that feeds on itself, that reinforces itself and rewards itself. You are going to learn as you teach, and learn as you touch. And the time has come to start.

Introduction to the Naked Body

Many couples will lie together in a naked or semi-naked embrace after they have had sex, and that certainly feels very good. But when was the last time you and your partner allowed yourselves to lie together naked in bed, snuggled up under the covers if the temperature required it, *without having sex*?

Most couples haven't been together naked in bed sans sex since the days they were dating. Do you remember those days? The days when you weren't afraid to slow your guy down? The days when your partner reassured you that he didn't want to have sex— that he only wanted to feel close to you? Those were some *very* hot days. Admittedly, very few of us ever mastered the art of lying together naked without having sex. Sooner or later, we lost our sexual willpower. But do you remember how exquisite it felt—even if it was only for a short while—to connect to your partner's warmth without feeling pressured to immediately start having sex? That feeling may have disappeared from your relationship a long time ago, when your sex life permanently kicked over into automatic pilot. But it is a feeling worth recapturing now, particularly because it will help you reconnect to something more primitive and vital that a man and woman should always feel in each other's naked presence.

Your First Assignment

Tonight, when you and your partner turn out the lights and go to bed, quietly take off all of your clothes before you slip into bed. Even if it is only for a few minutes, bring your body into full contact with your partner's body (have the front of your body snuggle up to the back of his body). It's okay if he is wearing his pajamas or sleep clothing—okay for now, at least. Now tell him you just want a few minutes to feel his warmth.

If your partner starts acting sexual, tell him that that really isn't what you need—you just want to feel close and connected. Be sincere, but firm. Now let yourself be with him, very comfortable but very still, knowing that he can feel your breasts and crotch pressing into him. Focus on the sensations of this intimate contact. Focus on your vulnerability and nakedness. Offer no additional explanations. Let him be there in bed with you, knowing that a naked woman who loves him is pressed up against him, hungry for his contact but not for his sexual acrobatics.

Three or four days after you have completed this assignment, repeat it a second time. But it is important that you let a few days pass to let the subtle impact of the experience fully register.

Your Second Assignment

Wait three or four days after you have repeated your first assignment, and then repeat it once again. This time, however, ask your partner if he would enjoy removing his clothes, too. Let him undress himself. Again, make it completely clear that you are not trying to seduce him—you just want to feel his warmth. Give him the option of being behind you with his groin pressed against your backside and his chest pressed against your back. In this position, you may feel his penis start to stiffen. Don't do *anything* but keep close contact. Enjoy the sensation, and allow him to enjoy the sensation without feeling pressured to take action. Let him see that he doesn't always have to perform. You may choose to drift off to sleep in this position.

After you and your partner have experienced "naked time" on several occasions, you may want to ask him to incorporate this into your weekly routine. Perhaps it is something you could do every Friday and/or Saturday night for at least ten or fifteen minutes. If it makes you want to have sex, that's okay, but you never want to turn this sensitive encounter into "the thing we do before we have sex." And regardless of whether or not you choose to have sex on occasion after your naked time, those ten or fifteen minutes of body contact must not ever become overtly sexual. You can feel incredibly sexual, and you can be having all kinds of erotic thoughts, but you don't want to turn it into a sex act (no masturbation, no penetration, no oral exploration). This is sensitivity training, not sex. There will be plenty of sex later.

Your First Subliminal Seduction

Through this experience of sensual contact, you are giving your partner several simple but powerful messages. You are telling him, "I want to be with you. I don't need you to be a pistol or a perfect stud. I don't need you to be in me and I don't need to get off. I just want to feel your body and have you feel mine. That is exciting to me; it is enough to make me feel good." You are also telling him that you have just taken the sexual relationship off automatic pilot. You are making it clear that you are not the same predictable partner with the same predictable sexual behaviors, expectations and needs. And that's a *good* thing, not something to be fearful of. You do not have to actually *say* anything; your actions are making these messages clear.

Your partner will respond to your covert messages by mirroring you, both in attitude and behavior. You open a new door; he will follow you through. You give him permission to be different and he will be different—he will go off automatic pilot, too. Up until now, he has been focused on the changes *he* has been going through—he may even be obsessed by these changes, and fearful of their consequences. But this is his very first experience of a change in *you*—a very different, positive change.

Your shift makes him feel as though something he is doing has opened a door in you. He feels you are responding to him, though he can't be certain what it is you are responding to. But you know exactly what you are responding to: the man you love is becoming the man you can't wait to make love to. He just doesn't know it yet.

Slowing Down Means Watching, Waiting and Feeling
Going off automatic pilot is an ongoing exercise in watching, waiting and feeling.

1. *Watching Your Partner with New Eyes*—Couples who have been together for a long time feel they could make love in the dark with their eyes closed. Most act exactly that way, even if the lights are on and their eyes are open. SLOWING DOWN means learning to see your partner and all of his subtleties.

2. *Waiting for Genuine Sexual Impulses*—Couples who have been together for a long time typically let the calendar or the clock tell them when it is time to make love. SLOWING DOWN means learning to respond to genuine sexual impulses, and allowing your body to express its sexual voice.

3. *Feeling Your Way Through Your Sexual Encounters*—Couples who have been together for a long time tend to have a highly choreographed sexual routine—a little kissing, little touching,

a little rubbing, a little screwing and call it an evening. SLOWING DOWN means breaking all routines and being in a unique sexual moment.

The remaining exercises in this chapter will help you start incorporating these three critical ingredients into the way you and your partner think, feel and act.

Seeing Your Partner with New Eyes
The next time you are going to make love to your partner, light three or four candles in the room where you will be and turn all other lights out. Don't consciously attempt to change anything else in your sexual routine, with one exception: Open your eyes to your partner.

I want you to look at and appreciate everything you see, making frequent, sustained eye contact and eye-body contact. Make sure that your facial expressions convey total acceptance and appreciation (and perhaps a little fascination). And don't turn away from him should he turn away. Watch him take his clothes off. Watch him as he moves toward you and looks at you. Watch him respond to your kisses, and your touch. Watch his penis swell and subside. Watch how he plays with you. Watch how he prepares himself to enter you. Watch him as he starts to thrust. Notice how this slows you down. And notice how paying exquisite attention to him actually slows *him* down. The difference may only be slight at first, but it will be noticeable, and you will feel more connected.

Repeat this technique at every opportunity—in *and* out of bed. Look at your husband every time he kisses you, touches you or takes your hand. It doesn't matter right now whether or not *he* is looking at *you*. He just needs to *feel* that you are watching. That will be enough to slow him down.

Observation and Reflection

Once you have become used to being a more focused, appreciative observer, I want you to start refining your skills by paying attention to the finer details of your lovemaking. The goal is to change from being an appreciative observer to being a *passionate* observer. This next exercise will show you how.

Slowly Writing a New Story

Imagine you are going to write a story about the way you and your partner make love. You need details, details, details. How do you know your partner is in the mood? What cues does he offer? Look for the subtle things—a change in his voice, a change in his manner, a change in his touch. Does he raise an eyebrow? Does he smile? Does he leer? Does he just grab you? How does he hold you? What, if anything, does he say? Does he let his touch linger? Do you? For how long?

Before you have sex, some clothing will have to come off. How does this happen? Who undresses whom? Is it button by button? Are things carefully folded or just tossed to one side? Do you undress separately and then scurry under the sheets to meet? Look for the details, and commit them to memory.

What happens next, and how quickly does it happen? Will there be much fondling, kissing, caressing, sucking or playing? Is he inside you the moment you reach the bed? Pay attention. Watch his breathing. Can you feel the changes in his heartbeat? Watch his eyes and his facial expressions. Listen for his sighs, for his moans and for the words he may use to let you know how he is feeling. Soak in this information to create a picture of this in your mind.

◘ ◘ ◘

Remember that if you are going to help your partner slow down to a speed where he will feel more sexually invigorated, you are going to have to lead the way. Sharpening your focus will naturally change your speed and the intensity of your response, creating a parallel shift in your partner. He doesn't need to know you are doing anything differently; the important thing is that he will *feel* it and naturally respond.

Consider writing down everything you have seen in a notebook or journal. This will be useful to you later.

Act Unnaturally

Now that you have become a more skilled observer, I want you to take what you have seen and start putting it to work. This begins by doing something I call "doubling up."

Whatever it is you and your partner do together naturally when you come together to make love, I want you to add the slightly unnatural element of doubling (unnatural only because you're not used to it).

- As you kiss, hold his kiss for twice as long; give twice as many kisses.
- When you reach for his hand or he reaches for yours, hold him for twice as long.
- If you are touching his shoulders, his arms, his thighs, his face or his hair, let your touches linger for twice as long.
- Take twice as much time to unbutton every button and unzip all zippers (yours *and* his).
- Take twice as much time to remove your bra and panties.
- Double the time it takes to pull his penis out from his underwear or pajamas.
- If you enjoy kissing or licking his penis, take twice as much time with this act.

Don't be self-conscious, and don't ham it up. Let yourself truly get lost in the longer moments. Finally, if you are going to have intercourse, take twice as much time to get into position. Nothing about your movements should seem too eager or rushed. Everything is slower, smoother and more deliberate.

Once you actually start having intercourse, proceed as you would normally. Do not try to lengthen that; this is not the goal right now. But even if you are both very excited, try very hard to keep doubling everything *leading* to intercourse.

If, at any point, your partner should ask, "Is everything okay?" be sure to assure him that you're just taking a little extra time to enjoy the connection. Then sit back and watch how he begins to change in response to your changes. Some men will ask after one kiss, others will never say a word, but all will experience the shift viscerally and respond by mirroring back some of the behavior.

A Loving Mirror

Most of us can get so caught up in our own pursuit of pleasure that we miss opportunities to let our partner know how connected we feel to him. This need not be done with words; as your next assignment demonstrates, a more powerful message is often communicated by sound.

This next assignment is actually an incredibly subtle mirroring exercise that requires your ability to focus on your partner (something we started developing in earlier assignments) and respond in a slow, controlled fashion (something we started developing in your last assignment). You cannot be an effective mirror if you are not paying exquisite attention and taking the time to reflect that back. Once again, your partner does not need to know you are practicing an exercise. In fact, it is better if he remains unaware—the results you obtain will be more genuine and powerful.

Following the Leader

Your goal in this exercise is to be a loving reflection of your partner's experience with you as the two of you are making love. You are going to accomplish this by subtly returning all of the sounds he makes during lovemaking with your own *slow* copy of each sound. It begins with his breath. When you hear him take a breath, gently take your own longer, slower breath. Let him feel your warm breath on his body or hear it close to his ear. If he moans or groans, return this with your own softer, slower moan or groan. If he makes *oohs* and *aahs,* copy them in your own soft voice, trying to stretch them out a little longer. If he uses words such as "yes" or "I love that," return his words with your own softer, slower version of those words. Don't try to sound like a parrot—he will become conscious of your behavior, or think that you are making fun of him. You need to be subtle. Keep your responses *understated*, even as you try to expand the time frame. Continue this through the course of your lovemaking until your partner has climaxed, giving him the clear sense that you have been "with him" through the entire experience.

A Gentle Introduction to a Gentle Transformation

Following a handful of the most simple and joyful assignments, you have already taken your first giant strides toward ensuring a long future of fabulous lovemaking. There have been no exhausting exercises, no complex new positions and no elaborate and intimidating techniques; and we've used no pills or gadgets. Yet something has already changed, and I know you can feel that change. You have opened a door, both for yourself and your partner, that will remain open for all the years you are together, if that is your desire. The door you have opened is one called possibility. And you have taken your first tentative steps right through. I believe in a simple, gentle approach to even the most complex sexual dilemmas, and I hope that with this approach, I am already starting to gain your trust.

3

Facts and Fiction After 50

I like to think of this chapter as "What to Expect When You're Expecting the Worst." If your partner is turning 50, or has already turned 50, you may have already fastened your seat belt and started bracing yourself for a very rough ride into your sexual future. You may already be expecting the worst as he ages. Yet so many of these expectations are not grounded in any kind of scientific or experiential reality. To the contrary, they are typically based on stereotypes, rumors, myths, misunderstandings and one big heap of fear.

Here is a simple fact: **Sexually speaking, women have *everything* to look forward to as their partners age.** I know this from both professional and personal experience. And I want *you* to know—to believe and embrace and be comforted by this truth. Yet I can't expect you to just take my word for this. You need to fully understand how I can be so optimistic about *your* sexual future. You need to be able to look into the same crystal ball that I look into—the crystal ball of hard sexual facts, real-life experience and understanding. So before I introduce any more exercises or techniques, let's take some time to alleviate your anxieties with the comfort of solid information. And the best way to accomplish this is to dive right into the pool of sexual *mis*information and disassemble the ideas and fears that hold women hostage.

———————◆———————

SEXUAL FICTION: *"An 18-Year-Old Male Is in His Sexual Prime"*

SEXUAL FACTS: You need to define your terms, and this is how *I* define "sexual prime": A man is in his sexual prime when he is a connected, responsive lover; as long as he stays connected and responsive, he remains in his prime. This should be your definition, too.

There is no question that men's sexual *efficiency* generally peaks between the ages of 15 and 21—typically, this is their most *physiologically* effective window in time. Vital hormones are at their peak levels; aside from an occasional case of first-time jitters, sexual equipment is usually functioning effectively with minimal effort; and enthusiasm knows no bounds. Yet these men are rarely *emotionally* effective; they are not yet emotionally connected and responsive. To the contrary, they can be embarrassingly *dis*connected. As pieces of sexual equipment, they may be as ready as they will ever be, and they may be hot and horny around the clock. But as *lovers*, they are not yet ready for prime time.

Would you really want to make love to an 18-year-old boy right now? I don't think so. You want to make love to the *man* you love—you just want him to be more "primed." You want him to have the enthusiasm of an 18-year-old, but the soul of a real man. With a little bit of guidance, and a few basic exercises, you and your partner can share your sexual prime right now. You don't need to turn back the clock—you just need to turn up the juice. The secret is not in the hormones, it is in his *and* your capacity to be more connected and responsive.

———————————⟨◦⟩———————————

SEXUAL FICTION: *"If My Partner Is Healthy and Active, He Won't Slow Down Sexually as He Gets Older"*

SEXUAL FACTS: *Most men will slow down as they age.* Although this often becomes obvious after the age of 50, it is really a gradual process that starts many years earlier (some would argue that it starts when a man is in his twenties). These changes are normal and natural, and have nothing to do with *you*.

Differences can appear in desire, overall sensitivity (which may decrease *or* increase), excitability (it may take longer, for example, for an erection to build), the need for stimulation, level of arousal, erection firmness, erection stability (intermittent loss of firmness), intensity of orgasm, orgasmic capacity, strength and volume of ejaculation response . . . just to name some of the most obvious. We'll discuss this in much greater detail in the next chapter, and look at some simple "solutions" (I use quotes because I don't think of these changes as "problems") that most men and women invariably overlook. For now, however, I think it's important that you know that as far as your partner is concerned, *none of these changes necessarily implies a lack or loss of enjoyment*—some actually produce increased enjoyment.

Being healthy and active doesn't stop the clock. But change is nothing more than a challenge—a challenge you will be prepared for by the time you have completed the exercises you will learn in this book.

SEXUAL FICTION: *"Loss of Erection Is a Natural and Unavoidable Consequence of Aging"*

SEXUAL FACTS: The myth of unavoidable impotence is probably the most widespread of all pieces of sexual fiction. The penis itself is not designed to suddenly stop functioning at a particular age, like an automobile part. Urologists agree that there is no physiological reason why any man will necessarily become impotent as he ages. And they don't encourage women to start worrying the moment their partners turn 50.

Yes, *some slowing down* is natural and fairly common. But *there is a big difference between slowing down and grinding to a halt.* Slowing down is a far cry from impotence. When the performance skills of the penis change dramatically, it usually reflects some other coexisting medical complication (such as poor circulation, excessive alcohol or cigarette consumption, weight problems, diabetes) or psychological complication (such as depression or anxiety). If the complication(s) can be addressed, sexual functioning is likely to improve.

So don't start drafting your sexual resignation letter quite yet—it may be another thirty or forty years before you even need to think about it.

SEXUAL FICTION: *"If You Don't Use It, You Lose It"*

SEXUAL FACTS: This is a great argument for having sex more often, and I don't want to discourage *that*. And it is important to acknowledge that regular use definitely keeps hormones flowing, hydraulic systems pumping, arms and legs flailing and loving hearts beating—all important contributions to sexual health. But there isn't much evidence to support the idea that an idle body becomes a nonfunctioning sexual entity. Actually, there is considerable evidence to challenge it, including a study I did at my own clinic.

Several years ago I did a study at my clinic with forty-seven men, ages 55 to 82, who had been diagnosed by their physicians as organically impotent. These men, on average, had not experienced an erection or intercourse with a partner in four to five years (minimum one year, maximum twenty-five years)—clearly a group that most women would be ready to give up on. Yet after eight or more treatment sessions involving sensual and sexual touching exercises (quite like the ones I will be sharing with you), all but *two* of the forty-seven men were having satisfying intercourse with orgasm. I know that sounds like a bit of a miracle, but it was really a straightforward response to simple techniques.

If these men could "come back from the dead," imagine the prognosis for a simple case of "less-than-perfect penis." The state of the penis is rarely one that is set in stone (no pun intended). It helps to think of sexual potency as a bear that can hibernate without losing its vital force (and that goes for women's potency, too).

<hr />

SEXUAL FICTION: *"Once He's over the Hill, He'll Be Losing Interest Fast"*

SEXUAL FACTS: Men do not lose interest in sex just because they age. Organic, hormone-driven sexual drive may change, as it may change for you. But sexual *desire* does not have to change dramatically, sexual curiosity does not have to change, playfulness does not have to change capacity for fantasy does not have to change and the experience of pleasure does not have to change—certainly not change for the *worse*. A man's turn-ons can change somewhat, but this is often a sign of emotional growth and greater sexual interest (e.g., when he is less turned on by pornography and more turned on by the feeling of closeness to his partner, I consider that *growth*).

Of course there are men who do seem to lose interest in sex as they get older, and right now your partner may be one of them. Sometimes this happens because the man is in a general rut, or because he is overwhelmed by demands, or because he fears his age, or because he is *feeling* his age fully for the first time. But here's a reality you need to keep in mind: Men are *most* likely to lose interest when they feel their partner has lost interest, or when they feel pressured, or when they feel inadequate because they are functioning less than perfectly. This loss of interest is not a life sentence—it is something that can be easily reversed with the help of a reassuring, genuinely enthusiastic partner who understands the physiology of men's changes.

SEXUAL FICTION: *"Sex Is Less Pleasurable for a Man as He Ages"*

SEXUAL FACTS: Many men report an *increase* in sexual and sensual pleasure as they age. For some, this increase is a direct result of slowing down and being increasingly "in the body." They report a heightened sensitivity to being touched, to being stroked and even to being hugged. Other men attribute their experience of increasing pleasure to the decrease in external stressors (child rearing, career climbing, etc.) and/or an increase in available time. The comfort and trust that evolve out of a long-term relationship also directly impact on men's experience of pleasure. Love and sex are not separate entities.

Don't confuse outward appearances (e.g., less frequent erections, decrease in erection strength and/or erection stability, decrease in volume of ejaculation, etc.) with his internal experience. Only your partner knows his own experience of pleasure. If a man says that sex for him is more gratifying than it has ever been, he is usually telling the truth.

———————— ‹○› ————————

SEXUAL FICTION: *"Impotence Is, in Most Cases, a Medical Problem That Requires a Medical Solution"*

SEXUAL FACTS: Emotional material gets in the way of sexual functioning. If a man is depressed, his equipment may falter. If a man is angry, his equipment may falter. If a man is completely stressed, his equipment may falter. If a man is overwhelmed, his equipment may falter. If a man has lost his confidence, his equipment may falter. I see this every single day in my clinical practice. The penis has a way of speaking up for even the most uncommunicative man.

It is my professional experience that these emotional complications have the potential to take a far greater toll on lovemaking than the natural consequences of aging. Before I share any new lovemaking techniques with *any* client, I always evaluate their "state of the heart." The mind-body connection should *always* be evaluated before trying to jump-start the penis with a pill, an injection or a surgical procedure. The only magic some couples need is a little bit of counseling.

I would never suggest that men's changes are always emotional in nature. As I have already stated, many physiological complications can affect how the penis does its job. I just have to wonder why it is so hard for the medical community to do *their* job in a fair and balanced way and acknowledge the potent influence of emotional factors on sexual performance.

———————◄○►———————

SEXUAL FICTION: *"Performance-Enhancing Medicine Is the Simplest, Most Effective, Most Rewarding Solution to the Aging Process"*

SEXUAL FACTS: Sexual miracles that come in pill form are still a highly experimental area of medicine. There are indeed many possibilities, but there are also just as many reasons for concern and caution.

Consider these facts, too:

1. Many men *can't* take performance-enhancing medicine.* For many men, there are serious health risks that outweigh the possible benefits. Yet these same men can also easily benefit from what you will learn in the chapters that follow.

2. Many men *won't* take a performance-enhancing medicine. Some are scared. Some are skeptical. Some can't afford it (this stuff is expensive!). Some are not interested. Yet these same men are likely to be very receptive to what you will learn in the chapters that follow.

3. Many men *shouldn't* take performance-enhancing medicines. For a significant percentage of men over 50, performance issues have a clear-cut psychological basis (depression, excessive anxiety, anger, grief, etc.) that needs to be approached from a psychological healing perspective. The failure of performance-enhancing medicines will only add to the psychological burden. Much of what you will be learning from me is both emotionally and sexually healing.

4. As I stated already in the first chapter of this book, a pill may give a man an erection, but it doesn't necessarily make him more sensual, more caring or more loving. To the contrary, it can *decrease* his

---

*PLEASE NOTE: *EVERY* man should consult his physician and carefully evaluate his personal risks before ever taking any of these medicines. Contraindications are serious and often life-threatening.

motivation to become a better partner, particularly if he is an erection-first thinker. And I think this is the greatest drawback of all.

You already know the reality: An uncaring lover with a formidable erection is still an uncaring lover. A clumsy lover with a formidable erection is still a clumsy lover. A selfish lover with a formidable erection is still a selfish lover. A boring lover with no imagination or playfulness can have a gorgeous erection, but he is still a boring lover with no imagination or playfulness. Pills don't change this.

SEXUAL FICTION: *"If a Man Can't Make Love, He Is Impotent"*

SEXUAL FACTS: The word *impotence* can mask a multitude of sexual realities and lead you away from a multitude of sexual opportunities. Many men who lose their ability to get an erection during lovemaking can still experience morning erections (waking with an erection), and can still give *themselves* an erection through masturbation. These men are *not* impotent, though clearly certain sexual channels are blocked.

There are many potential obstacles on the road to an erection. Fear is a huge one, particularly among men who are getting older and losing their sexual confidence. Anger is another. The physiological demands of intercourse—being more complex than the demands of masturbation—are another. A change in responsiveness to a partner's method of stimulation is yet another. And the list goes on. Too often, the word *impotence* is tossed around at the first sign of change. Then the word becomes the biggest roadblock. When a man is experiencing changes in his functioning, it is vital to resist labeling those changes, and imperative to investigate *all* possible contributing factors—including partnership issues. Often there is a surprisingly simple explanation and an equally simple remedy.

———————— ◇ ————————

SEXUAL FICTION: *"There Is No 'Male Menopause'"*

SEXUAL FACTS: Both men and women still have a hard time fully accepting any menopause that is not the property of a woman. But when we manage to put our stereotypes aside, we know that there is ample evidence demonstrating that men have their own dramatic version of this "change of life"—a change that can begin even before the age of 50.

Here are some of the male menopause basics. For starters, there is an overall slowing down of the body—it may be so gradual that it is almost imperceptible, but it is still happening. Testosterone levels may decrease, lessening the sex drive, and the testicles may also shrink slightly, diminishing the production of semen. Even if testosterone levels remain constant, there may be changes in the body's ability to use testosterone efficiently. Mood swings are typical. There may also be a change in other hormones, including growth hormone and DHEA. (DHEA is the natural hormone that helps the body make testosterone. It is often hailed as a magical anti-aging chemical that revs up testosterone production, but I must acknowledge that I haven't seen a lot of good clinical evidence to support this.)

And there's more. Sense of smell becomes less acute, making men less responsive to subtle sexual cues such as pheromones (our "sex" scents) and other body scents, clearly affecting the turn-on process. Weight gain, fatigue and sleep disturbances reflecting internal changes are not uncommon, and these changes affect desire and responsiveness.

That's a *lot* to give men pause. But perhaps what makes men pause most is something else entirely: the questioning process that begins in middle age as men start to reevaluate their value and potency in the world: "Am I losing my edge in the marketplace?" "Will I soon be replaced by a younger, stronger version of me?" "Am I employable?" "Am I desirable?" "Am I all washed up?" This questioning process can have a huge impact on a man's sexual desire and performance, particularly if his partner is not sensitive to these issues.

Add it all up and a very unsettling picture emerges—a picture of male menopause that, in many ways, is more complex, more confusing and potentially more overwhelming than female menopause!

Maybe you will never be able to talk to your partner about male menopause—unfortunately, most men are still not talking. But talk is not the only remedy. Knowing the facts will keep things in perspective for you, enable you to be more supportive and, I hope, stop you from ever blaming yourself for something that is all about *his* physiology, *his* experience and *his* fears. (In Recommended Reading you will find a list of required reading for any woman seeking more information about the emotional and physiological complexities of male menopause.)

SEXUAL FICTION: *"An Aging Penis Is an Insensitive Penis"*

SEXUAL FACTS: As men age, sensitivity of the penis may decrease or *increase*, and more men report the latter. The penis may look less alert, but it may actually be feeling far more complex sensations of pleasure. Increased penis sensitivity tends to encourage a man's transition from being very intercourse-driven to being more contact-driven— i.e., more interested in experiencing the sensations of physical contact that come from touching, rubbing, stroking, kissing, licking and sucking. The shift doesn't mean your partner is suddenly bored with intercourse—more likely, he has found something exciting and new that has captured his attention. Heightened pleasure leads to more participation, more curiosity and more motivation to prolong sexual connection.

An aging penis is often a more appreciative penis. When it comes to judging the sensitivity of the penis, looks are often deceiving.

———◦———

SEXUAL FICTION: *"The Penis Starts to Shrink After 50"*

SEXUAL FACTS: Long before George Costanza brought national attention to the shower "shrinkage" controversy on the classic episode of *Seinfeld*, older men and their partners were observing these changes *out* of the shower and taking mental notes. But the facts tell us that a cold shower produces far more shrinkage than a fiftieth birthday party.

Most shrinkage in older men is actually an optical illusion created by the build-up of fatty tissue in the pubic mound (the area directly below the waist surrounding the penis). Sometimes an inch or more of a man's penis can "disappear" into the pubic mound. The effect is enhanced or diminished, depending on whether he is standing up straight, bent over forward or lying on his back. The best remedy for this is a healthier diet, some tummy-tightening and some physician-recommended cardiovascular exercise. Interestingly, for some men, the penis actually appears to get *longer* as the years pass. This is due to the stretching of ligaments in the pelvis.

Though the penis may indeed lose a bit of its length as a man gets much deeper into his golden years, the testicles are actually the first thing to truly, and irreversibly, shrink in size. This is part of the male menopause package. Shrinkage of the testicles does reduce the production of semen. This is something most men and women *do* notice, and often worry about.

But the decrease in semen production is natural, and not necessarily a sign of poor health.

―――――――――◦―――――――――

SEXUAL FICTION: *"Men Are Always Ready to Have Sex—If They're Not Ready, Something Is Wrong"*

SEXUAL FACTS: The mind may always be ready for sex, but the flesh can lose some of its ability to cooperate. After orgasm and ejaculation, men go through a "rest-and-recovery" phase referred to as the *refractory period.* As men age, the duration of this time-out generally increases, and after 50 this becomes more obvious. What may have taken thirty minutes just a few years ago (and thirty seconds thirty years ago) now may take a few hours, or even longer. This does not mean your partner is losing interest in sex, it just means he needs more physiological down time ("don't even think about it" time). Most men will not act sexual during this resting phase because they lack confidence in their ability to have an erection and/or orgasm. Their reluctance may even carry forward for several days. But this shying away should not be misinterpreted as a loss of interest or a serious problem. And it can be minimized with a concerted effort to minimize sexual pressure and encourage playfulness. (We'll talk about this more in chapter 8.)

———————◄○►———————

SEXUAL FICTION: *"A Penis Is a Penis Is a Penis"*

SEXUAL FACTS: No two men are the same, and no two penises are the same. The implication of this myth is that a penis is not terribly complicated and that it will continue to function pretty much the same way it has always functioned throughout the course of a man's life—i.e., it will get erect, it will ejaculate with sufficient stimulation and it will contract until it gets erect again. This objectification of the penis stops a woman from seeing its unique characteristics, its unique responsiveness, its unique needs (yes, the penis has needs!) and its unique pattern of change.

It is completely unrealistic to expect the penis of a 50-year-old man to have the same responsiveness or performance characteristics as the penis of a 20-year-old man. And it is equally unrealistic to expect the penis of a 50-year-old man to function and respond the way it did when that same man was in his twenties. Such comparisons only discourage and add to sexual pressure. Men and women have to be prepared for changes. Nothing about our sexuality is static.

If you want to learn how to make gorgeous love to your 50-plus partner, you have to learn about the unique personality of his penis.

———————◄○►———————

SEXUAL FICTION: *"Change Is Around the Corner"*

SEXUAL FACTS: Now that I have started preparing you for the many changes that *might* happen to your partner after the age of 50, I need to tell you about the many changes that might *not* happen. Fifty is not necessarily "the magic number." Your partner may not start showing obvious signs of slowing down until he is in his sixties, his seventies or his eighties. And, believe it or not, some men *never* show obvious signs of slowing down. It depends on genetics, emotions, lifestyle, habits and a whole lot of luck. This doesn't mean that the body isn't changing; it just means that these changes are so slow and subtle that they are not significantly affecting his sexual interest or ability.

What will happen to *your* partner, and *when* will it happen? I couldn't know. But I do know how to prepare you for all possible scenarios, and that is what this book is all about. Instead of "waiting for the inevitable" start focusing on how you can make love, and keep making love, to a man over 50.

Summing Up

It's important to clear away the bad information if you're going to make room for the good, and we've started to do just that. How many stereotypes have you been carrying with you into the bedroom? How much unnecessary worrying have you been doing? How much misinformation have you been keeping in storage? And how have these stereotypes, the worrying and the misinformation already crept into your lovemaking? Stop and think about that for a few moments. Now prepare for the shift.

Your partner's sexual transition is filled with potential. Your partner may become a *different* lover as he grows older, but, theoretically speaking, he should become a *better* lover as he grows older. Yes, your experience of lovemaking may change as his body (and your body) changes. But the most critical element in making love is the connection two people have with each other—a connection that should be so much more rich and vital with every year you are together.

Your partner's physical capabilities are not deteriorating, they are simply changing. And with myths and misunderstandings out of the way, both his physiological and emotional capabilities are primed for real growth. In the next chapter we'll explore some of these physiological changes in greater detail, and experiment with a few simple solutions to everyday snafus.

4

The Temperamental Penis

I am getting older, and my penis is not getting any harder.
—Robert M., age 61

Most women expect their partner's penis to *always perform like the good soldier—firm, erect and ready for active duty at a moment's notice.* For years they have experienced their partner as willing and able, and if anything, they have marveled at how little work it takes to get a man fully aroused. So it is usually quite confusing when their partner passes the fifty-year marker and the performance of the penis becomes less consistent and less predictable.

Because most women have little or no understanding of how a penis functions, a man's changes can present a real challenge to the relationship. Neither partner welcomes the shift. The man is often just as confused. And he is certainly not happy to see "Old Reliable" become so temperamental. The issue of virility comes into question. The issue of desire comes into question. Even the issue of mortality can come into question.

Here's something that is going to surprise you: There are five important factors that are responsible for the majority of these changes in penis performance, and impotence is *not* one of them. These five factors— the five culprits that often sabotage lovemaking after 50—are **circulation, stimulation, lubrication, stress** and **sleep,** and they are the focus of this chapter. As you will soon learn, the impact of these five factors ("The Big Five") is not set in stone. To the contrary, that impact is something you can easily control—there are many remedies for even the toughest problems.

We're going to talk a lot about the penis in this chapter—its many talents and its many transitions, its foibles and its "smarts." We'll start with a short course in mechanics and plumbing, then continue with a little bit of penis psychology and a refresher course in technique and timing. Then, with this new information, we'll take a fresh look at "the facts of life after 50" and the impact of the "Big Five." What does it mean when the penis is rock-hard? What does it mean when it suddenly falters? What does it mean when it is completely unresponsive? And what makes its behavior so unpredictable? Why is the penis temperature-sensitive? Why is it pressure-sensitive? Why does something that feels so good on a Thursday seem to feel so bad on a Sunday? Can *you* make a difference if *his* penis is temperamental? Is it all in the hands of the gods? By the time we have completed this chapter, you will have the answers you need.

Meet His Penis

For the past ten, twenty, maybe even thirty or forty years, one of your best friends in the world has been your partner's penis. You have watched it swell, shrink, rise and fall; you have felt it throb and explode. But how often, during those years, have you stopped and wondered who this friend of yours really is? You count on your partner's penis to bring you pleasure and to bring your partner pleasure. Yet for most of your life, you have probably taken it for granted. While you have, I'm sure, remained thankful that it exists and that it works so efficiently, you have let it remain one of life's little mysteries.

The days of living in the dark are over. Making love to a man over 50 means turning on the lights, pulling back the curtain and viewing the workings of this all-powerful giant. What *is* the penis? What is it made of? How does it work? These are questions that need to be answered if you are to walk into your sexual future with confidence and clarity. I don't want you to *do* anything to your partner, or with your partner, before you know why you are doing it. And if you are worried that lifting the veil will take away the magic and make your experience of sex too clinical, I assure you that just the opposite is true: Lifting the veil will ensure that magic continues to be possible.

Let's start by establishing what the penis is *not*.

• *The penis is not a muscle.* Though it may sometimes look like one (it can look so strong!), feel like one (especially when it's hard) and act like one (when, for example, it appears to flex), the penis is not a muscle. You probably already know this, but it still can be confusing. It is even confusing for most *men,* who insist that the penis often feels *just* like a muscle—a muscle they can't control. This is certainly why so many men, in spite of knowing better, treat the penis like a muscle, and try to exercise it like a muscle in the hope that it will grow larger and stronger. Alas, it does not respond.

• *The penis is not made of cartilage.* It is nothing like your nose or your knees. Perhaps that surprises you. It surprises a lot of women who try to comprehend the soft, yet also firm "split personality" of the penis—an inherent contradiction that is so visible and, on occasion, frustrating.

• *The penis is not a bone.* It has no bone in it. And, other than its nickname (nodding to its ability to become fairly straight and firm), it has no true bony characteristics—no tissue structure similarities. I'm pretty sure you knew this one, but I needed to state it for the record.

So what *is* the penis? The penis is actually three long cylinders of non-muscle tissue bundled together with the urethra by a fibrous sheath. Wow. I just said a mouthful.

Let's deconstruct that sentence, starting with *fibrous sheath*. The fibrous sheath (*tunica albuginea of corpora cavernosa*, for those who find science sexy) is the cover that holds everything together and in place. It's a semi-elastic cover that can expand as its "contents" swell. The fibrous construction of the sheath is what gives the penis its firmness when it expands. But, being only *semi*-elastic, there is a clear limit to how much it can expand, the same way there's a clear limit to how much stuff your can put in your handbag before it starts to come apart at the seams. And that is why popular penis-enlargement devices never seem to deliver on their promise. Thanks to the fibrous sheath, penis length is, essentially, predetermined by the sheath-maker.

The *urethra*, as you probably know already, is a hollow tube through which both semen and urine will travel along their way to being expelled at the tip (head) of the penis. That's a fairly simple one. Before it is expelled, semen manufactured in the testicles actually collects first in the urethral bulb, which is located below the prostate. It is then propelled through the tube when the bulb spasms, with the assistance of a muscle that runs from the base of the penis back to the anus. This "helper" is the *pubococcygeal muscle,* also known as the *PC muscle.* Perhaps you are familiar with this muscle already, as it is a muscle you and your partner have in common. The PC muscle has a direct effect on the force of a man's ejaculation, and on the strength of his sensations of orgasm, and we *will* be attending to this very real muscle later in our program.

That leaves the *cylinders of tissue.* Of the three long cylinders bundled together with the urethra inside the fibrous cover of the penis, two are of the same tissue composition, and the third has a slightly spongier composition. (Want some more Latin? The twin cylinders are the *corpora cavernosa*—they run along the sides of the penis; their spongy big brother is the *corpus spongiosum,* which runs all the way to the head of the penis.) All three cylinders are fed by a rich network of blood vessels, and that's the important part. Because when a man is sexually excited, these vessels fill with blood, swelling the cylindrical tissues and creating an erection.

For blood to flow into these cylinders, smooth muscles located at the base of the penis (not part of the penis itself) have to relax. This is one reason why muscular tension created by stress, intentional squeezing or even unintentional squeezing due to lack of awareness is an erection-killer. Relaxation is vital. The blood that flows into the three cylinders is then trapped by valves at the base of the penis that close in response to the pressure, and the erection is secured. Inside the sheath, it actually looks like three erections. But all you see is one lovely erect package.

Circulation and the Temperamental Penis

An erect penis is a penis that has filled to a state of firmness with an infusion of blood. It has nothing to do with cartilage, bone or muscle. It's all about blood. **Erections depend on blood flow.** If there isn't enough blood in the penis, there isn't enough erection. Period. This simple piece of information may not sound very sexy or very interesting, but it really should, because it is going to help you solve the riddle of the temperamental penis.

In the world of real estate, they say that there are three things that matter most: location, location and location. In the world of the sex therapist, it's circulation, circulation and circulation. *Anything* that affects blood flow to the groin can affect a man's erection. Anything. Think about that for a few moments. Try to imagine how many different things can interfere with blood flow to the penis. Position. Temperature. Friction. Gravity. Sudden movements. Physical pressure. Digestion. Blood pressure. Cardiovascular health. Drugs. Alcohol. Illness. And that's just for starters.

When a man is young, it sometimes seems that the blood flows efficiently to the penis against all odds. Not snow, not rain, not sleet, not hail—nothing seems to slow that blood down. If he has only a pint of blood left in his body, it manages to collect in his penis. And presto, the perfect erection. But as a man starts to age, the behavior of his penis begins to reflect the subtle and not-so-subtle changes in blood flow. The penis actually becomes a more accurate barometer of a man's internal state—of his emotional health and physical health. It actually becomes more honest, and vulnerable.

Go with the Flow

Circulation, circulation, circulation. That explains why it may be easier for a man to get an erection when he is standing up straight than when he is lying in bed in the "push-up" position with blood rushing to his hard-working arms—if a position is better for blood flow to the *groin*, it's better for his erection. It explains why it's harder to get an erection on a full stomach (and you thought it was your cooking!)— blood is being diverted to the stomach for digestion. It explains why erections are affected by blood pressure medications. It explains why it's harder for a man to get an erection when he's standing on his head or hanging from the chandeliers. It explains why cardio-vascular exercise directly impacts on sexual vigor. It explains why it may be easier for a man to have an erection first thing in the morning when the body is well rested and circulation is most powerful, and it explains why he may fail to get an erection late in the evening when the body is fatigued. It explains why muscle tension in the thighs, hips and buttocks weakens an erection (the muscles actually steal blood from the penis). Circulation explains a lot of things. And I haven't even talked about the more complicated stuff, like the valves that are supposed to trap the blood once it has collected in the penis. Those valves don't work perfectly forever, either (we'll discuss that more in chapter 7).

Can you see where I'm going here? I'm trying to make it clear to you that when you are making love to a man over 50, you have to become more circulation-conscious, and you have to help raise your partner's consciousness, too. **Try to forget about complex, invasive solutions to temperamental penis behavior and start looking for simple solutions.** Simple adjustments to maximize circulation can yield *huge* results. Startling results. And we'll talk about some of those adjustments at the end of this chapter.

The Pathways to Excitement

Let's talk a little bit about excitement now. Excitement is all about nerves, and there are actually two pathways in a man's nervous system that lead to sexual excitement. Mother Nature was generous. Both pathways involve the spinal cord. One pathway requires the enthusiastic participation of the brain. The other is, essentially, brainless. Let's focus on the brainless one first, and try to keep the jokes to a minimum.

As you have probably noticed more than a few times in your life as a woman, an erection can be produced from touch alone. Woman touches penis, penis responds. Short and to the point. End of story. This immediate and inspiring response is possible because there is a reflex nerve pathway between the penis and the lower spinal column (we call this the *reflexogenic pathway*). All that is required is the right touch. That touch sends impulses to the spinal cord, and the erection instructions are wired back in the blink of an eye. No thought involved. It's almost magical. Do notice, however, that I said the *right* touch. We will learn more soon about right and wrong. **When it comes to touching the penis, there is definitely a right and a wrong way to touch, and that becomes more critical after the age of 50.**

The second pathway is more complex. It is called the *psychogenic pathway* because the brain is actively involved. When a man thinks about sex, fantasizes about sex, sees a sexually provocative figure (real, in print, or on film) or has some other brain arousal, nerve impulses from the brain travel down the spinal cord, collect in the "erection center" in the lumbar section of the cord, continue traveling to the sacral area of the spine and then go out to the penis with instructions to start the erection process: "Get busy!"

What gets so very complicated here is that *negative* thoughts and associations can be just as powerful, if not more powerful, than the positive ones, creating chaos in this system, and more temperamental penis behavior. **Emotions can blaze the trail to erection, or just as easily block the trail.** And their effects are not consistent.

When we talk about performance anxiety, we are talking about a problem along the psychogenic pathway. Stress, anger, fear, sadness—all of these can short-out the system, and all the right stimulation in the world may not be enough to get the penis back on line. This is the *emotional* component of the erection process—the component that is often overlooked until a couple finds their way into the office of a competent therapist or counselor.

Who's in Control?

We have already established that the penis is not a muscle, a bone or an assembly of cartilage. Well, there is something else the penis is *not*: It is not under the direct control of its owner.

Erection is not a voluntary process. A man can hope for an erection, pray for an erection, stimulate himself like crazy to produce an erection and beg his partner to help, but he cannot *force* an erection into existence. That's just not how it works, and women need to really be clear about this. In this sense, the penis truly has a mind of its own—two minds, actually, because it responds to nerve impulses from two different pathways in the body. And, as every man will concur, **the harder a man tries to force his penis to become erect, the less likely it is to happen**—adding stress aggravates penis shutdown. This challenge becomes more and more obvious as a man gets older, and it can be a source of confusion, embarrassment and anger for the stubborn and the undereducated.

A man who tries to control his penis is one very frustrated man—a man who isn't willing to understand and accept how the penis works. And a woman who thinks that her partner is in control of his penis, or, even worse, thinks that *she* is in control, is also lacking insight into the complexities of this fragile organ. "Penis attitude" inhibits penis performance. Every woman needs to understand this. We'll talk more about *your* penis attitude in chapter 6. For now, embrace this lesson: **You can't force your partner to get an erection, and you can't demand an erection. You can only facilitate the possibility. Trying to control your partner's performance will only bring out more temperamental behavior.**

Also start thinking more about *subtle* sexual pressures you may be conveying to your partner.

• If your sexual expectations have not changed in twenty years, *this is subtle sexual pressure*—your partner is changing, but you are not making it clear to him that you are happily adjusting to those changes.

- If you expect your partner to figure things out on his own, *this is subtle sexual pressure*—he's not the only one who is changing, you are *both* changing, and the relationship is changing.

- If you don't make your needs clear, *this is subtle sexual pressure*—your partner's imagination can fill him with stress.

- If you don't talk about sex, *this is subtle sexual pressure*—somebody has to open a partner dialogue, or internal dialogues take over your sexual relationship.

Help your partner have a clearer mind. When the mind gets in the way, sometimes all hell breaks loose. And sometimes it can freeze the body solid—every part of the body, that is, except the penis. The penis gets frozen *soft*. It is part of the body's natural fight-or-flight stress response. We are just not physiologically built to make war and make love at the exact same time. Stress is not an aphrodisiac.

Woman Touches Penis, Penis Responds

The reflex pathway—the path that does not directly involve the brain—is the erection path of least resistance. The main ingredient here is direct physical stimulation—pleasurable stimulation. And it is important to emphasize the word *pleasurable* because the wrong touch at the wrong time simply will not get the job done.

In my professional life, I have met very few women who have committed themselves to learning and refining the kinds of touch that consistently bring pleasure to their partner. Let's face it: If we use our sexual history as the teacher, it is easy to conclude that it doesn't take a whole lot of sophisticated stimulation to help a man's penis get hard. Touch the zipper on his jeans, his penis gets hard. Pull his belt from a single loop, his penis gets hard. Slide your hand up his thigh and softly squeeze his testicles, his penis gets *way* hard. Sometimes it seems as though all a guy needs is a good strong breeze to make his penis hard. Such immediate cooperation from the penis does not encourage women to learn the art of touch. Why obsess over something that seems so superfluous? Everything works, the guy seems perfectly happy . . . why ask too many questions?

But as a man ages and Old Reliable starts to show its years, the erection process is not quite so simple. The reflex pathway remains intact—direct touch still stimulates the penis—but the *quality* of that touch becomes far more critical. What once felt absolutely fine can now feel strange, insufficient, awkward or even bad. Being touched is no longer enough. The man needs to be touched in a more specific way, at a more specific pace, for a more specific length of time. His requirements become very well-defined. And this is all very confusing for you, particularly because your partner is probably not communicating any of this to you in any direct way. Instead, he is far more likely to be trying to work with whatever you are offering him, trying to make not enough feel like just enough. He doesn't know how to introduce this new information into the lovemaking equation without rocking the boat.

Many men have reported to me that as they age, they lose faith in their partner's sensitivity to their specific needs for stimulation. Gradually, these men come to feel as though they are the only ones who know how to touch themselves in a way that maximizes their erection potential. But what has really happened is that their needs have *changed*, and they don't know how to make their partner a part of those changes. Many of these same men acknowledge that they have subtly, or not-so-subtly, incorporated self-touch into their lovemaking to ensure that they will have the erection they require. There is nothing wrong with this, from a sex therapist's point of view. Yet the shift leaves a lot of women puzzled, feeling inadequate or feeling left out. "Is my partner a closet masturbator who has come out of the closet," we wonder, "or is something wrong with *me*?"

Learning to Touch, Again
I know that you have handled your partner's penis for many years, and it's hard to imagine that you need to be reeducated. But that is exactly what I'm suggesting, and I'm hoping you won't feel insulted or judged.

If you are like most women, you have never learned enough about stimulation of the penis, and there's nothing to be ashamed of. You haven't *needed* to know. But that is changing, and it will continue to change as your relationship continues to grow.

I speak to so many women who are afraid of their partner's penis: afraid to hurt it or afraid to do something wrong. This fear creates a tentative touch that can be less than satisfying as your partner's needs for stimulation change. The penis is something that must be embraced with love and confidence, not fear. So if you can put your beat-myself-up voice and your sensitive ego both to the side for just a few minutes, I ask you to consider the following suggestions and instructions.

Handling a man's penis effectively requires a sense of surefootedness (surehandedness?) that, of course, only comes with lots of practice. So the first thing you need to do is find more opportunities to get that practice. Make a decision to actively incorporate touching into your lovemaking ritual. No more "kiss kiss, squeeze squeeze, put it in me please." It is time for you to take control.

It Takes Two Hands

Pleasurable stimulation of the penis usually requires a fairly firm grasp. Not a death grip. But a firm grip. This doesn't mean I want you to firmly grasp the penis the instant you see it—a few moments of light playfulness are always an appropriate icebreaker. But if you're going to melt that ice, you need to eventually add a little more muscle.

Most women fear the strength of their own hands, yet you probably are misjudging your own strength. What is *not* always exciting for a man is what I call an "angel's touch"—a touch so light and delicate that the man is straining to feel stimulated. When a man is incredibly excited, an angel's touch could be enough to bring tears to his eyes and swelling to his groin. But when he is in need of some serious stimulation, as is more often the case after the age of 50, you must go where angels fear to tread.

The first thing I recommend is: *Work with both hands*. Using both of your hands gets you *involved*, and your partner needs to feel that you are involved— involved and excited. Most women are used to using only one hand to stimulate their partner. Typically, the woman is lying on one side and working with the more free, more available hand. But getting involved means not lying down on the job. *You will probably need to sit up* so that both of your hands are free, and so that you can clearly see what it is you are doing. And a little bit of light will also help.

What will you *do* with that second hand? You have many options here. One possibility is dedicating your second hand to the stimulation of his testicles. Yes, careful handling is in order here—his testicles are quite sensitive to your touch. But gentle squeezing and massaging of the testicles can add an extra dimension to your stimulation that may be exactly what your partner needs. Handle with care, of course, because you definitely *can* hurt him. But don't be afraid to . . .

> . . . slowly explore the soft skin with your hands,
> . . . snugly cradle the entire sack in your hand, or
> . . . lightly roll the testicles against each other.

Start slowly here, particularly if this is very new for you. You need to have a sense of his sensitivity range. Pay very close attention to your partner's response, including the direct response of his penis. Your partner *will* let you know what feels good. If it's too much for him, he will certainly make that clear. And if he wants more, he will try to cue you, even if he is not yet comfortable asking you directly. Listen to his moans—he may be moaning because it feels good, but this also may be his way of encouraging you to continue without specifically verbalizing his request. Pay attention to the rate of his breath, looking for signs of pleasurable tension as well as discomfort. Most of all, watch the direct feedback you are getting from his penis, the great communicator. If the penis appears to be stiffening, it is responding to something you are doing. If nothing is happening after considerable effort, vary your touch.

A lot of women enjoy using their second hand to explore various parts of their partner's body. They will use that hand to wander between his testicles, his thighs and the skin that leads from the testicles to the anus (the area where you can actually feel his PC muscle twitching). Contrary to popular fiction, men have more than just *one* erogenous zone. Use your second hand to discover areas of particular sensitivity. Perhaps he enjoys having his buttocks squeezed; perhaps he enjoys the touch of your hand on his lower abdomen. You can only know by experimenting. Don't let your touch become too fearful, apologetic or feather-light. Experiment with firmness, and watch for feedback.

Some women devote their second hand primarily to stimulation of the penis—both hands working in pleasurable unison. As the penis starts to swell, you can have one hand at the base and one at the head; or both hands overlapping, concentrating on the shaft. If your partner has never experienced you using both hands to massage his penis, this will make him feel like a sultan. A man does not have to have a ten-inch penis to enjoy the attention of both his partner's hands. There is something both flattering and exciting for a man to receive this much physical attention. The important thing is that both of your hands are working together. The stimulation needs to be coordinated—slow and even, gradually building. What you don't want is a touch that is tentative, frantic, schizophrenic or careless.

How Much Is Too Much?

How firmly can you grasp the penis? How hard can you rub? These are critical questions. As always, it depends on the man, and the best way to find out is to dialogue with your partner directly. Even with much dialogue, however, it will still require a continuing process of trial and error to find his maximum response on any given day. What feels great on a Thursday night in July may feel overwhelming on a Saturday morning in August; what feels underwhelming at 3:00 A.M. may feel absolutely perfect at 9:00 P.M. You know how this works. The two golden rules are *sensitivity* and *adaptability*—you have to keep paying attention, and you have to be prepared to change the program day to day, month to month, and year to year. Bear in mind that what is likely to be unpleasant at *any* time, and very quickly so, is excessive *friction* on the skin of the penis.

Going from Soft to Hard

Even if your partner is very excited and enthusiastic, his penis may still be soft at first. When your partner was younger, it probably seemed as though his penis was *never* soft—not when it was anywhere close to you. But now the erection process is not as instantaneous and consistent. This means you will be having more contact with a half-erect or even completely flaccid penis at the start of lovemaking. Don't let this confuse you, discourage you or turn you off. When the penis is soft, it is still very sensitive and responsive, and all forms of physical contact can feel quite pleasurable. Give the erection process a chance to unfold. Take the penis in your hands and slowly start to massage it. This needs to be a loving, patient massage, not a "rush, rush, where's the erection?" massage. Your direct, consistent stimulation will start the flow of blood that is required for the build-up of an erection.

As the penis firms up, you want to move your hand(s) up and down the shaft. If your hands are not lubricated, you want to hold the soft shaft skin that envelops the penis snugly enough so that it moves *with* your hands; you don't want the skin rubbing *against* your hands, creating friction. I'll say that again:

If you are not using lubrication, the soft skin of the shaft should be moving up and down with the movements of your hands. That means you need to be holding the skin fairly firmly—not so tightly that you are pulling it taut like the head of a drum, but firmly enough to make it move with your hands. Most women do not hold the shaft firmly *enough*. The firmness of touch that you require when rubbing your clitoris or vagina is typically a fraction of what *he* requires. This is a very common mistake that women make, gliding with a light touch instead of grasping with a firm touch. And this lighter gliding actually creates more friction, and potentially soreness and "burn" to the skin as the gliding becomes more vigorous.

Let your entire hand(s) get involved. Many women use only their thumb and forefinger to grasp the penis, circling the penis with a little "o." Yet many men find this "two-digit" approach to holding the penis to be lacking, both in style and substance, as their need for stimulation becomes more intense. More fingers give you more strength and more surface area for pleasurable stimulation. They also give the message that you are not afraid to take firm hold of his penis and give him exactly what his penis needs. An apologetic, tentative touch does not feel very good to a man who needs consistent, controlled stimulation from a confident partner.

Going to the Head of the Class . . .
The head of the penis does not have the same freedom of movement as the skin of the shaft, and needs to be handled quite differently. The foreskin, if it is present, is quite elastic, but the head itself is composed of a more taut, sensitive surface. The head may appear to be more fearsome, but it is actually far more sensitive than the shaft, and requires greater care. Most men assert that the top two inches of the penis, including the head, is the area where most erotic sensation is derived from, and the area that is most hotwired for orgasm.

Lightly touching, massaging and playing with the head is likely to be highly stimulating for your partner. Still, too much direct rubbing or pulling may be painful. What usually feels best for the man is a longer stroke that starts along the shaft and moves the skin of the shaft to the rim of the head—or just past the rim—and then back down the shaft.

On the underside of the penis, where the head of the penis joins the shaft, is an area of utmost sensitivity. Try to make contact with this area as you slide your hand up the shaft of the penis and over the rim of the head. Rubbing this sensitive juncture can be especially pleasurable for a man, and typically, it will facilitate his orgasm. But depending on his level of arousal, stimulation here can also become *too* intense, and actually be experienced as a negative. Think of what it feels like when your clitoris gets too much stimulation from an overzealous partner, and you'll know what I'm saying. So approach this area with special care, and pay really close attention to the impact of every bit of contact you make. The "ridge" that runs down the underside of the penis from the head to the base (it usually looks like a large vein) is also slightly more sensitive than the rest of the shaft, and a grateful recipient of special attention.

All the Right Angles

Another thing you need to become more conscious of is the angle at which you hold your partner's penis as you are stimulating him. As the penis becomes erect, most women tend to hold the penis at a ninety-degree angle to the body—straight up in the air (if he's lying down)—when they stroke it. That's fine. But you may

get better results if you hold your partner's penis so
that it is pointing a little bit up, toward his *stomach*,
rather than straight out. Pointing the penis down,
toward his legs, is the *least* stimulating angle. Up
slightly toward the stomach, out straight, but not
down—this is very important.

In the ninety-degree and "up-angle" position, the
valves that hold the blood in the tissues of the penis
seem to function most effectively, keeping his erection
consistent. In the "down" position, more blood seems
to flow out of the penis and back into the rest of the
body, making a consistent erection harder to maintain. The valves at the base of the penis require a
certain kind of pressure to stay closed, and the
mechanics of the down-angle position may fail to provide this necessary pressure. Experiment with the different angles and see if this is true for your partner.

We Need to Talk About Lubrication

Most women would never consider using lotions, oils,
creams or other kinds of over-the-counter lubrication
on their partner's penis unless they needed it to facilitate intercourse. They don't think of lubrication
(aside from a bit of saliva, perhaps) as a part of foreplay, or they are turned off to the idea of it. Yet when
it comes to working with a temperamental penis,
lubrication is nothing short of magical. If you're trying to live your sex life without the regular use of
lubrication, you're simply missing the boat.

Lubrication—*generous* lubrication—is the key to bringing a temperamental penis to life, even a very tired penis, or one that is getting on in years. With generous lubrication you are free to fully massage the penis without being fearful. And even the slowest stroke delivers a wealth of sensation. You don't have to worry about holding the skin of the penis just right, or tugging on it just right. Your hand(s) can glide up and down the penis, mimicking the sensations of intercourse, without fear of generating an unpleasant degree of friction. The very same motion that has the potential to create so much discomfort without the use of lubrication now becomes the motion of choice. You can exert more pressure, and you can use a more powerful manual stroke. And the vast majority of men find all sensations infinitely more pleasant. With *less* effort, you are providing greater "constructive" stimulation (i.e., stimulation that leads to erection). For many men over 50, this one ingredient is all that is required to jump-start an entirely new experience of their own erection.

Are All Lubricants the Same?

For years, the word on the street, as well as in the library, has been that saliva is the best lubricant for foreplay. Saliva *is* an excellent lubricant, and I have no interest in challenging that basic fact. Yet a lot of women feel that producing a constant and generous supply of saliva is too much work. Saliva dries quickly, it does not always flow freely and one application is usually not enough. If you are serious about learning to massage and stimulate a temperamental penis, you need to find a lubricant that is *not* temperamental. There are so many products on the market today that are made expressly for lovemaking. These products work, though some do work better than others, and the only way to discover what feels best for you and your partner is experimentation.

The world of intimate lubricants has exploded over the past few years and your choices may seem overwhelming. There are foams, oils, gels, creams and water-based products, all of which work, though the results will be different for each. There are many flavored lubricants on the market—cherry, strawberry, piña colada, even chocolate!—which can be fun to play with, but most tend to become tacky fairly quickly and loose their "glide." I suggest you find a good basic lubricant first. Professional masseuses like to use baby oil, and this is a good choice if you are going to be experimenting with your touch. But I don't like this choice if your penis massage is going to be followed by intercourse. Better to find a lubricant that is both man-friendly and woman-friendly—something that is specifically recommended for sexual applications, not for babies' bottoms. Many of my clients are most comfortable with a water-based product manufactured under the name "Wet-Lite" that is available in novelty shops, catalogues and some pharmacies. I am not endorsing this product, but if you are wondering where to begin, this is as good a choice as any. And please note: NEVER USE A LUBRICANT ON THE GENITALS THAT WARNS IT IS NOT FOR GENITAL USE.

The important thing to remember when using lubrication is to be generous with the product. Once applied to the penis, most lubricants will ultimately thin and lose their loose and easy glide. The solution is simple: Apply more, and do so as often as necessary. Pay attention to the changes. You can tell when more is needed from the way your partner's penis feels in your hands. If your strokes are not smooth and easy, it's time for more. Don't think of using lubrication for a one-time application, the way you would use it just prior to intercourse. When you are giving attention to a temperamental penis, be prepared to spoil it with lubrication. Of course, you always want to pay attention to the feedback from your partner.

Preparing for Your Orals

It's time to talk about oral sex. I don't know how comfortable you are with the thought of kissing, licking and sucking on your partner's penis, and I don't want to scare you, pressure you or turn you off. Even though oral sex has been "out of the closet" and a subject of celebration for a very long time, it may not be your personal favorite. Perhaps oral sex is something you don't even want to think about . . . ever.

Perhaps it is something you can't get enough of. Most likely, you fall somewhere in the middle. But I'm sure you have been wondering where oral sex fits into this new equation I am presenting.

You must believe that I am not being paid by an all-male sex lobby to make the following statement: Oral sex works magic on the temperamental penis. I wouldn't be a good sex therapist if I ran away from this one. Think about it: Wet, warm, sliding, gliding—this stuff feels too good! It certainly feels good for him—it's why so many men have worshiped Linda Lovelace. And it *should* feel good for you, too. Now, you may have had experiences to the contrary—many women have. But with a loving partner, and with you in *complete* control at all times, it is a great tool to have in your sensual fix-it kit.

Oral sex is not the only way to excite a temperamental penis, and I don't want you to think this is something you must do. But it is a powerful way to stimulate the erection process. If you are open to the idea of it, we should review some of the basics.

It helps to think of your partner's penis as a delicious, big lollipop that you can't wait to taste, suck on and roll around in your mouth. (No biting through to the chocolate center!) Once again, the idea is to be generous with the use of lubrication—in this case, the natural lubrication of your saliva. *Get the penis wet and keep it wet*, remembering that the head is far more sensitive than the shaft. Your mouth should be able to freely slide over the penis. Don't force yourself to take more into your mouth than you are comfortable with. If you are only willing to suck on the head of the penis right now, that's fine—take in whatever you can handle. If you are only willing to lick the shaft with your tongue, it's still a start. Use your hand(s) to make up the difference, massaging the rest of the penis with the saliva from your mouth. Let that saliva flow.

If you need additional lubrication to keep your hands and mouth soft and your movements smooth, consider using an edible lubricant to supplement your saliva. But . . . DO NOT USE COMMERCIAL LUBRICANTS THAT ARE UNSAFE FOR ORAL CONSUMPTION . . . not if you are having oral sex. If you need to switch to a non-edible commercial lubricant at any time, you must wash your partner's penis thoroughly before you put it back in your mouth. I recommend keeping both a wet and a dry washcloth by the bed.

As with manual stimulation, slow and steady motions are usually best. Avoid frantic movements, forceful movements and uneven rhythms. Keep it slow, steady and wet. Licking the penis up and down, licking the testicles, and licking other sensitive areas close to the penis are also quite effective for stimulation. Stay away from anything too aggressive, such as "love bites," unless you know your partner is comfortable with this. Pay attention to the response; let it educate you. You may have known your partner for dozens of years, but there is always something new to learn about his penis. After all, he's still learning, too.

When you are comfortable with your technique, try these variations:

1. If your partner is lying down, rest your face on his abdomen so his penis is angled up toward his stomach as you suck it. The warmth of your face and hair will provide additional stimulation.
2. Kneel in front of him while he is standing up and suck on his penis while he continues to stand. Remember that standing is ideal for circulation. Doing this near a mirror—where you can watch, he can watch or you both can watch—is even more stimulating.
3. Lie on your side or on your back, allowing him to remain standing, or let him straddle your shoulders with his knees, bringing his penis to your mouth.

Above all, please remember at all times that *your* enjoyment is critical. If you can't get absorbed in the process, and don't genuinely feel pleasure from sucking on your partner's penis, you may be better off working with just your hands.

Wake Him When He's Ready
The Scenario: You come home late from a party and you're feeling incredibly romantic and sexual. You

wrap your arms around your hunk of a guy and he tells you that it's way past bedtime.

The Scenario: You wake up in the middle of the night with an overwhelming urge to make love. Your hands start to explore your partner's crotch; half-awake, he pushes you away. You get a little more persistent and he gets annoyed.

Yes, these could both be *relationship* problems. But more than likely, they are *sleep* problems.

The last thing I want to talk about in this chapter is the impact of *sleep* and *rest* on the temperamental penis. When a man is in his late teens and early twenties, no time seems like a bad time for sex. It can be the middle of the afternoon or the middle of the night—if there's an opportunity for sex, he is there firing on all cylinders. Raging hormones and youthful energy seem to know no bounds.

But then the years pass, and you start to notice the effects of sleep, or the lack thereof. A bad night's sleep, a short night's sleep, stressful sleep, disrupted sleep, chronic tiredness—all of these can create a problem for your partner's ability to get an erection and keep that erection. The body needs sound and sufficient sleep, night after night, for the penis to function at its best. Yes, many men can put in a hard day's work in spite of their need for more rest, but the penis needs to be more pampered; in the absence of consistent, adequate sleep, be prepared for skittish behavior.

Most men in this country do not get enough sleep. That is an established fact. But what has not been studied enough is the loss of sexual functioning in our sleep-deprived culture. Your partner needs sleep. When he is full of energy—first thing in the morning, for example—he will feel his sexual vigor. When he is tired, his penis will be temperamental. When he is exhausted, he may have no interest in sex at all. This is all very normal and appropriate. And it is something you need to be more conscious of as you plan your sexual future.

Sleep and stress, stress and sleep—they torture each other in a vicious cycle. And with every passing year, the typical man watches his stress account go up a little higher and his sleep account drop a little lower. Before you buy your partner a bottle of Viagra for Valentine's Day, think about the quiet contributions of stress and sleep. Of course you're tempted to consider the quickest fix. But maybe what your partner really needs is a better pillow or a decent nap. Are you tempted to wake him in the middle of the night for a quickie? Your heart is in the right place, but he may not be able to get anything of *his* in the right place. Sometimes there is no substitute for a good night's sleep.

Stimulation, Circulation, Lubrication, Stress, Sleep (AKA "The Big Five")

Think about these five words the next time you think about making love to the man you love. Think about these five words every time you look at his penis. And let them reorganize your approach to making love.

Without giving you any complex exercises, I have already given you your most important tools. I have given you a new way of seeing your partner and understanding the temperamental behavior of his penis. Of course, there is much more to discuss. His orgasm. His ejaculation. His fears. His fantasies. And, of course, *you*. But look at what you have learned, and think about how you will be able to apply this new information directly to your world.

You are developing different eyes. Expert eyes. Diagnostic eyes. As you look at your partner through those eyes, wondering about the future of your lovemaking, here are the questions you will be asking yourself:

1. Is circulation an issue here?
2. Is stimulation an issue here?
3. Is lubrication an issue here?
4. Is stress an issue here?
5. Is sleep an issue here?

Stay open to these five possibilities, and half your work is done.

Putting in the Fix After 50: The Home Remedies

When it comes to lovemaking, I never encourage women or men to look for a quick fix. That's because I know from experience that most women and men will either look in the wrong direction, or overlook important underlying issues. But once you are tuned-in to the impact of circulation, stimulation, lubrication, stress and sleep on the temperamental penis, much fixing does happen rather quickly. And to conclude this chapter, I would like to give you a number of practical applications for everyday lovemaking (twenty-one, to be exact) that accommodate the information you have learned thus far. I call them my home remedies. You may want to call them your "twenty-one-gun salute."

Remedy #1: Change your lovemaking schedule *now*. If your partner is at his best before bedtime, make that "your time." If he seems stronger and more fully functional in the mornings, don't keep waiting till bedtime. If you don't like the morning lighting, close the curtains. Don't be a creature of habit.

Remedy #2: Look for new positions that maximize blood circulation to his penis. Let him stand up during sex, or kneel by the bedside. You can find many comfortable, gratifying positions for yourself at the edge of the bed. Don't always force him into the "push-up" or missionary position.

Remedy #3: Always have your favorite lubrication by the bedside before lovemaking starts. Don't wait to see "whether or not we'll need it this time," and don't wait till the moment before insertion. Have it ready from the beginning, and use it generously from the beginning.

Remedy #4: If you are going to be on top while making love, pay more attention to how the weight of your body pressing on his groin may be cutting off circulation to his penis. Use your arms more actively to support your weight and minimize pressure.

Remedy #5: If his erection window is narrowing (he does not stay hard for as long as he used to), don't start stimulating him aggressively until *you* are ready for intercourse. Let the foreplay focus on *you*. This will take the pressure off *him*.

Remedy #6: If his erection takes more time to build and stabilize, give him that time before you have him enter you. Don't race. Don't make love unless you have the time to make love.

Remedy #7: Have your sex *before* meals, especially before *big* meals. Haven't you noticed how the best-laid sexual plans seem to evaporate by the end of dinner? Big meals slow the body down as blood is diverted to the digestive system. You want as much blood as possible diverted to his genitals.

Remedy #8: Pay attention to the rhythms of his body. At what times and on what days does he seem to be most invigorated? When is he least invigorated? Start orienting your lovemaking around those days and times. Having good sex every Saturday afternoon is better than having mediocre sex two nights a week. Having good sex once every two weeks is better than having mediocre sex every week. Less is often much more.

Remedy #9: Don't just lie there, *do* something. Don't wait for his erection to show up, use your hands and/or mouth to bring it forth. And let lubrication be your little helper and do the hard work for you.

Remedy #10: If you both want to make love, but you know he's tired, encourage him to take a twenty-minute nap. Even this little bit of sleep can recharge his battery and facilitate the erection process.

Remedy #11: Don't ask him, "What's wrong?" Use your information to help make things right.

Remedy #12: If you want to eat before you make love, encourage him to have a smaller meal. Discourage him from eating enough food to knock himself out. You can both fill your stomachs later, after you've filled your hearts.

Remedy #13: Don't rush things. Remember that with age, it may take a little more time for his penis to fill with blood. Give him that time, and do everything you can to assist the process.

Remedy #14: Minimize the acrobatics and stick with uncomplicated positions that provide good, consistent circulation.

Remedy #15: Don't keep changing positions once you've started to have intercourse. If he's standing up, let him remain standing. If he's lying on his back, let him remain there. Every time you change positions, you change the flow of circulation. That can be very disruptive to the erection process.

Remedy #16: Minimize distractions. Minimize time-outs. You need a protected window for lovemaking. Stress and erections don't mix.

Remedy #17: Pay attention to your geometry. The penis typically has an easier time staying erect (the tissue holds the blood more effectively) when it is angled up or out, not pointed down. To achieve a good angle, you may need to place a few pillows under your bottom during intercourse, or get on your knees and arch your back.

Remedy #18: Practice in the off-season. Experiment with your touch by giving your partner nonreciprocal massages. Tell him you want to learn more about what makes him feel good. If intercourse is on the agenda, he may have trouble relaxing—take that burden off him.

Remedy #19: Watch the thermostat. Cold temperatures and cumbersome covers are not very freeing for the penis.

Remedy #20: Help him relax. If you sense that his muscles are tight, touch those muscles with your hands and tell him to relax. Perhaps a fuller body massage would help him. Sucking in his gut is a particular no-no—it locks up all kinds of muscles. Give him permission to let go. Remember, blood does not flow well into the penis when muscles are tense.

Remedy #21: Don't panic if his penis is less than perfect. Remember, neither one of you is in control.

Notice how I haven't said anything about lingerie. Or dirty movies. Or sexy talk. Or wild fantasies. Believe me, there is a place for all of these, and they are all fabulous and exciting in that place. But erotic and exotic solutions are only appropriate once you have attended to the basics: circulation, lubrication, stimulation, stress and sleep. Erotic and exotic alternatives are a poor substitute for fundamentals, and missing the basics only increases frustration and pressure. Right now, this is where you need to stay focused. The rest will all come later.

5

Sexual Fitness
and the Full Penis Workout

In this short chapter we are going to focus on a handful of very specific "penis exercises" that I hope you and your partner will get started on right now. I use quotes because we won't actually be exercising the penis. We will be exercising and invigorating the area of the groin immediately surrounding the penis—an area that is directly responsible for many crucial aspects of penis performance. We know the penis is not a muscle, so there is no way to directly exercise it. Yet we *can* exercise and build important supporting muscle tissue, and we can also learn how to stimulate blood flow to the groin. Both of these techniques can have an immediate and obvious impact on erection, orgasm and ejaculation.

As you read through this chapter, you are going to notice right away that many of the "penis exercises" require very active participation from your partner. Some exercises are actually solo exercises designed just for him. This means that there is no way to get most of this chapter's work done without your partner's enthusiastic contribution. And I can hear some of you groaning already.

The exercises in this chapter are feel-good exercises that men truly enjoy. They are incredibly simple and surprisingly sexy. Yet I know, even as I am writing this, that some men will have little interest in anything that requires a consistent commitment. Or perhaps they will experiment for a while, but lose interest quickly. As a sex therapist, I'm a little spoiled. The men who come to my office are eager to work, and keep working. They want great lovemaking more than *anything*. But I also know that is not always the case in the outside world. We all live very busy lives, and the thought of any new daily exercise regimen— even the simplest, most pleasurable one—often feels like too much of a demand. Your partner may *want* great lovemaking, but he may not be ready for any work.

If your partner is not open to these exercises, don't be discouraged. They are only part of a much larger program that is in your control and already well under way—a program that cannot be sabotaged. I have included these exercises because I know there are many men who *are* ready to take a more active role in laying the groundwork for their sexual future—for these men, the following exercises will yield powerful results. But there are other ways for a man to get involved in his sexual future without performing these specific exercises. So do what you can, then continue to the next chapter. By the time you have integrated everything else I am presenting to you into your lovemaking, your partner may very well have had a change of heart. Positive results generate interest and enthusiasm.

Phase I: The Daily Massage

What do you think of when you see the word *massage*? Do you immediately start to relax? Does a smile come to your face? Do you see the pleasure gates opening? I hope your partner has the same response. But it doesn't really matter, because *this* massage is not just about pleasure, it is also about business: the business of blood circulation. And this is a deal your business partner can't refuse.

The following massage is no ordinary massage—it takes only five minutes a day, and it is specifically designed to enhance blood circulation in the groin. It may be very pleasurable, but it is not a sexual massage. It may be very simple, but the effects of this massage are quite complex, and often noticeable within a few weeks. The important thing is that it is done *daily*.

The Technique

Here's how it works. Every day (either in the shower or in bed) you need to firmly massage *around* the base of your partner's penis with slow, consistent strokes for approximately *five minutes*. Use your first two fingers and gently press or rub around the base of his penis as if it were the face of a clock and you were traveling around it in circles. You are not massaging the penis or the testicles (not even "by accident"), only the surrounding area—primarily the pubic mound and inner thigh area. It is very important that your partner remains completely relaxed during this five-minute massage. His thigh muscles, abdomen muscles, groin muscles and PC muscle (we'll talk more about this one in a minute) need to be fully relaxed the entire time. If you are doing this as a couple, pay attention to those muscles and let him know immediately if they seem tense. Remember, tension inhibits blood flow.

To minimize the possibility of arousal, your partner may prefer to do this massage by himself, particularly because it is something he needs to find time for daily. But it is fine for you to participate, as long as no one deliberately tries to make this sexual. *This is not an arousal exercise.* You'll both get used to this fairly quickly as long as this is understood from the very beginning.

If the massage is being done in the shower, use liquid soap to get smooth, firm contact. If your partner is lying down in bed, some kind of lotion or massage oil should be used. Keep a towel by the bed to keep things from getting messy. You may prefer to put a towel underneath his buttocks.

◼   ◼   ◼

What you are doing with this massage technique is "awakening" the tissue and muscle at the base of the penis through which blood must flow to the penis during the erection process. Invigorating this area enhances circulation, bringing health and "youth" to this vital area. This has a direct bearing on the effective functioning of the penis. Circulation, circulation, circulation. Remember?

If the stimulation from the massage occasionally creates the desire to have sex, that's okay. But only *very* occasionally. Turning this into a sexual exercise defeats its purpose because it creates a covert—or overt—sexual demand. As soon as there is a demand, one or both of you will quickly become reluctant to participate every day. This exercise needs to be done *every day*. So treat it as a nonsexual exercise—an easy, pleasurable, very important, *non*sexual exercise—even if it means encouraging your partner to go it alone.

This massage technique is a "lifer"—something your partner should attend to, with or without your assistance, every single day for the rest of his life. But results don't take a lifetime. They are, in fact, fairly immediate. In two to three weeks your partner will start to feel (and see) . . .

- a change in the strength of his erections, particularly his morning erections, and
- a change in the length of time it takes for his penis to go from being flaccid to being erect (we call this period of time the *latency period*).

You and your partner may also notice that he is able to stay erect longer, and that the strength of his erection is more consistent. All from this one very simple and pleasurable massage technique.

What About *Your* Massage?

A lot of women learn about this massage and then start asking, What about *me*? Can five minutes a day do something for my body, too? Absolutely. Massaging your pubic mound and the inner thigh tissue and muscle surrounding the vagina may be the invigorating wake-up call you need, too. You may experience more erotic sensitivity in the area, higher levels of arousal and even stronger orgasms. It's certainly worth experimenting. Many women enjoy making this a daily couple's workout with both partners self-massaging simultaneously or taking turns massaging each other. As it is with any exercise regimen, your involvement is certainly going to be motivating to your partner.

Phase II: Mastering the PC Muscle

It is now time to learn more about the pubococcygeal (or pubococcygeus) muscle. The pubococcygeal muscle—PC muscle, for short—is actually a group of bundled muscles that runs from the pubic bone to the tailbone, in both men and women. If there is one bundle of muscles that can make a difference in the next five decades of a man's lovemaking, the PC muscle is that bundle. It can have an equally dramatic influence on a woman's experience of physical pleasure, but we'll talk much more about that in chapter 9. Right now, we're going to focus on *him*.

A man's PC muscle is his key to the kingdom—it is the one muscle that can singlehandedly begin his sexual transformation after the age of 50. There are many paths to the top of the mountain of enhanced sexual performance, but the PC muscle is the shortest distance between the bottom and the top.

- Mastering the PC muscle changes a man's ability to get erect and stay erect.
- Mastering the PC muscle changes a man's ejaculation control, ejaculation force and ejaculation volume.
- Mastering the PC muscle changes a man's experience of orgasm.
- Mastering the PC muscle gives a man the opportunity to become multi-orgasmic.
- Mastering the PC muscle feels really darn good.

How is all of this possible? It is possible because the PC muscle is a multifunction muscle intimately involved in the processes of orgasm, ejaculation, urination and, in a more passive way, erection. Due to its location and strength, the PC muscle has a direct impact on many aspects of male genital functioning. The muscle that stops the flow of urination from the bladder is the PC muscle (you should know that from your experience with your own PC muscle). The muscle that "lifts" the testicles, makes the penis appear to twitch or makes it appear to momentarily swell is the PC muscle. The muscle that helps move semen out of the urethral bulb and up through the shaft of the penis is the PC muscle. And one of the spasming muscle sensations men experience during orgasm is the PC muscle spasm. As I said: many functions, one muscle.

There's only one problem, and it is not a small one: Mastering the PC muscle takes some work (just like a woman's PC workout—the so-called Kegel exercises—takes some work). First your partner has to find it, isolating it from other muscles in the groin area. He has to strengthen it with exercises. And he has to maintain that strength with a short but regular program of exercises. This will take a few minutes every day. But if your partner is motivated, and ready to experience a sense of power and control (dare I use the word) that has always been ungraspable, the remaining pages of this chapter have been written just for him.

For Men Only: The PC Pep Talk

Getting your PC muscle in shape is a simple, pleasant process that requires only a few minutes of concentration every day. These are isometric-type exercises that you can perform while lying in bed, sitting at the breakfast table or driving to work. No clothing needs to come off, no creams or lotions are used. Once you begin the first exercise, you will begin to notice physical results very quickly—sometimes within a few days. Emotional results will be apparent even sooner—these exercises are going to make you feel stronger, sexier, more tuned in and more hopeful about the future of your lovemaking as soon as you start them.

Now you may be thinking, "I'm not eighteen anymore. Exercise or no exercise, my penis is not going to function the way it did when I was a young guy." I understand the thought, but that's not likely to be the reality. With PC muscle strength and control, you may develop a relationship with your penis that is more gratifying and less frustrating than anything you have experienced to date. You may develop a sense of confidence, understanding and control that you've *never* had. A healthier, more "conscious" relationship with your penis is also bound to dissolve performance anxieties and fears of losing potency. Think about how these issues are affecting you right now, and have the potential to influence you even more in the future. And think also about your most important relationship: the one you have with the woman you love. This relationship has the most to gain.

It doesn't matter if you are 50 or 70—PC muscle training gets impressive results. The PC muscle is a muscle, plain and simple. It works and responds like any other muscle, and it can be strengthened like any other muscle. And every man who is willing to do the work can bring his PC to a state of readiness within just a few weeks. After that, it's a simple maintenance job that takes only a few minutes each day. We're not talking about hours in the gym here; we're talking two or three minutes at home in bed, a very small investment with limitless return.

For Men Only: Isolating the PC

Before you start to work on the PC muscle, you must first find this muscle and isolate it from other muscles in and around the groin. For a small percentage of men, this is very simple—perhaps you are one of these men, confidently squeezing your PC right now. On the other hand, you may feel a bit uncertain—this is far more typical. Many men are completely unfamiliar with the various muscles in this part of the body, and easily confuse the PC muscle with their buttocks muscles, thigh muscles or stomach muscles. For some men, the entire area feels like one large, undifferentiated mass of muscle. This is particularly true for men who are not exercise-prone.

The PC muscle is the muscle you squeeze during urination if you need to stop the flow, or squeeze out a few last drops. It is the same muscle that can jiggle the testicles or cause your penis to throb. To accurately find this muscle, place one or two fingers right behind your scrotum. Pretend that you are urinating, and try to stop the flow. If you are in the bathroom, it may be easier if you actually do start urinating, then try to stop the flow. That muscle you just flexed to cut off the flow of urine from the bladder is your PC muscle. Did you feel it momentarily tighten? Did you also notice or feel your testicles slightly "jump"? This is the muscle you're looking for. Squeeze it again, keeping your fingers in place and feel the muscle tighten once more.

When you squeezed your PC muscle, did your stomach, thigh and/or buttock muscles also tighten? This is very typical, but not helpful for PC strengthening. Squeeze your PC again, this time being more conscious of keeping your stomach, thigh and buttock muscles completely relaxed. Remember that you're not interested in getting an erection right now, only in squeezing the PC muscle. So don't let your hands or thoughts wander too far into sexual terrain. Focus on the muscle.

For Men Only: PC Reps for Beginners

Now that you've found the PC muscle, it's time to start the workout. For the first few days, all you really need to do is squeeze the PC muscle on occasion and let go. I just want you to see how it feels and get used to that feeling. After a few days, start a more serious workout. Slowly squeeze and let go, *twenty times in a row, three times a day.* Squeeze, release, repeat . . . twenty times. Wait a few hours for the muscle to rest and then do it again. Wait a few hours and do it once more.

If it helps to keep your fingers on the muscle right now for focus and feedback, do it. You want to be sure you're squeezing the right muscle. After a week or so, you probably won't need the assistance. Of course, if it motivates you to keep your fingers there because it feels good, you can keep them there *every* time you work out. It's like having a spotter there to monitor your progress. You can even have your partner use *her* fingers to help you. She might enjoy being part of your process.

As it is with every muscle exercise, proper breathing is important. You don't want to hold your breath. You need to breathe freely as you squeeze.

For the next ten days, establish a simple but consistent daily PC regimen of twenty squeezes in a row, three times per day.

PC Troubleshooting
PC exercises come with two potential pitfalls . . .

- The first and most common mistake men make is overzealous exercising.

- For some men, discovering the PC muscle is like finding a new toy. They just can't get enough of it, until they strain it by pushing too hard. You must go slowly at first, as you would with any other muscle exercise, and let the muscle build. Follow my guidelines—don't create your own. We will build the workout in increments. For now, you need to be patient and trust the professional. Avoid PC burnout.

- The second mistake many men make is failing to completely isolate the PC muscle and contaminating their workout with stomach, thigh or buttocks flexes.

- A contaminated workout yields poor results. Stomach muscles, thigh muscles and buttock muscles need to be *fully* relaxed when you are working out the PC. If you are a tummy-tucker, you've got to let that gut out during your exercises. Lying down or sitting in a comfortable chair will help the thigh and buttocks muscles relax. Use one of your hands to continually check these muscles for tension, or ask your partner to check for you and give you feedback.

- If you are having real problems with muscle contamination, the best solution is to exhaust the problem muscles before you start your PC workout. Let's say you have a tendency to squeeze your buttock muscles during the workout. Before you turn your attention to the PC, tighten and release your buttock muscles ten or twenty times. This will help sensitize you to muscle differences, and also tire them just enough to get them out of the way. You would do the same thing with your stomach or thigh muscles if these were your problem muscles. Should you need to do more pre-squeezing—say thirty or forty reps—that's fine. Does this sound like a lot of work? I understand. But we're only talking about a few *days* of work. If you are diligent, within a week's time you will have solved the contamination problem, and you'll be free to focus on the more important goal: PC power.

For Men Only: PC Reps, the Second Step

After ten days of PC exercise, you are ready to slightly modify the program. You are still going to do twenty squeezes a day, three times a day. But now you need to hold each squeeze for a full one-second count before you release. Squeeze, hold for one full second, release. Do this for five days. After five days, increase your hold count to *two* full seconds. Squeeze, hold for two full seconds, release. Continue this for five more days, practicing three times a day. If you like the result, increase your hold count once again—this time to three full seconds. Do twenty repetitions, three times a day. At the end of this time period, your PC muscle will be in pretty good shape. However, you should continue to exercise your PC muscle every day (for the rest of your life)!

Erections and the PC Squeeze

When it comes to orgasm and ejaculation, a powerful PC muscle works wonders. But what about erections? The PC muscle is intimately involved in the erection process, too, yet not in a way that very many men would imagine. While squeezing the PC can actually cause a momentary throbbing in the penis, giving the short-term sensation and appearance of penis stiffening, the PC actually *interferes* with erection development and erection stability when it is subject to constant squeezing. I need to say that again: *The PC muscle interferes with both the creation and stability of your erection when the muscle is subjected to constant squeezing.* It does wonders for the experience of orgasm and ejaculation—something you'll learn more about in chapter 8—but it sabotages erection.

As men age, and begin to lose confidence in the strength and stability of their erections, many try to compensate by squeezing the PC muscle constantly during sex. Knowing that they can't really force an erection, they try to force it anyway by squeezing the PC muscle. And the longer they have intercourse, the more they squeeze. Because it is the only muscle that *feels* like part of the penis, the belief is that a PC death grip will keep the penis hard. It *feels* like it should help. Many men imagine that it *is* helping; they imagine that pumping this muscle is like pumping blood directly into the penis. Yet the reality is the complete opposite: PC squeezing is taxing a hydraulic system that is designed to work in a very different way.

For an erection to build, blood must flow freely into the penis. We have already established that. Tensing muscles cuts off blood flow to the penis. We have established that, too. And tensing the PC muscle is no exception. There is no "pump" in the groin. And although this squeezing may create a momentary sense of power and possibility, it actually hampers the build-up of an erection, while also encouraging an existing erection to falter. Muscles need to be relaxed for blood to flow into the penis, and for the necessary valves to close. And the most crucial muscles are those closest to the penis: the buttock muscles, the stomach muscles, the thigh muscles and the PC.

If a man wants to learn to build his erection, he must learn to *relax* all of these muscles—*particularly* the PC muscle. And that is what these PC exercises are all about: isolating and strengthening the muscle so you have complete control. You need to be the master of your PC muscle so you can squeeze it when it will bring you additional pleasure, and *relax* it when you want to stop it from interfering with the erection process. You have started to master the squeeze—it is time to master the release.

For Men Only: PC Release, the Crucial Third Step

You are going to continue your PC squeezes every day—twenty squeezes, three times a day. But we need to add one last element to the exercise—an element that focuses on the release.

Squeeze your PC muscle and hold it for a full count of two seconds. Now relax the muscle *slowly*—not abruptly, but bit by bit, as though you were slowly unclenching a fist. This release should take place over a full three-second count. So it's squeeze, hold for two full seconds, then gradually release to the count of three. Nothing should be abrupt. You're trying to create smooth movements the way you would create smooth movements doing bicep curls in the gym. Squeeze, hold for two full seconds, release to the count of three. Squeeze again. Do this twenty times, three times a day. Add this to your daily PC workout that you intend to continue for life.

Where Do We Go from Here?

PC mastery opens many doors. I will take you through some of these doors later in this book, particularly in the chapter on orgasm and ejaculation. PC muscle strength and control are also the secret to male multiple orgasms—yes, men can have multiple orgasms, too! If you want to learn how to use your newly acquired PC fitness to trigger male multiple orgasms, I encourage you to read my book *How to Make Love All Night*. You have already completed the hardest work, and discovering your capacity for multiple orgasm is like discovering a new sexual universe.

But the time to bring your PC control into your regular lovemaking is right now. When you are making love, make a commitment to being PC-conscious.

- Keep the PC muscle group completely relaxed as your erection is building and notice how much easier it is for your erection to build.
- Once you have a good erection, notice how keeping the muscle relaxed during thrusting makes it easier to maintain that erection.
- Notice also the changes in intensity in your orgasm and ejaculation.

Commit yourself to your PC workout—twenty reps three times a day—and you will reap the benefits for the rest of your life. Now please hand this book back to your partner—she needs to get back to work.

6

Harsh Words, Healing Words

Sexual intimacy has been my vocation for more than fifteen years, and it has been my passion for almost twenty-five years. If there is one thing I have learned again and again through both professional and personal experience, it is that the biggest roadblock to passion and pleasure is neither technique, timing, experience, performance nor the firmness of a man's penis. It is *attitude*. His attitude and *your* attitude.

Fear. Shame. Negativity. Anger. Misinformation. Lack of flexibility. Closed-mindedness. These are the enemies of sex. Yet each and every one of us carries some of this into the bedroom.

As your partner passes the fifty-year milestone in his life, he is going to become increasingly sensitive to his changes—both the subtle and the not-so-subtle. He will be monitoring these changes, and he may worry about these changes. But your partner is going to be equally if not more sensitive to *your* reactions. If you treat every small shift like it's the end of the world, he'll *feel* like it's the end of the world. On the other hand, if you make it clear, both in your words and your actions, that it's no big deal, he'll be able to reach the same conclusion. You have a lot of influence here—you have a lot of power. More than you may even know, your pleasure is his concern. And your attitude is the key to that pleasure.

In chapter 3 we looked at some of the common stereotypes clouding the issue of sex and aging. In this chapter, we need to look at personal attitudes—your attitudes—that may be making it difficult or impossible for you to have the thing you desire most: a loving, exciting, gratifying sexual relationship with the man you love. To do this, we need to examine some more sexual fictions, and replace these thoughts and beliefs with accurate, constructive information that will heal sexual rifts and open your world to a loving and exciting sexual connection.

THE ATTITUDE: *"A Real Man Has Real Erections"*

THE REALITY: A *real* man has all kinds of erections, depending on his mood, his diet, his health, his attitude, his sleep schedule, his stress, his fantasies and the position of the moon (not to mention circulation, lubrication and stimulation).

It is incredibly destructive to equate the hydraulic properties of a five-inch piece of tissue with masculine identity. Yet men do this to themselves constantly, and women do it to the men they love. As you have already started to learn, the physiological process of aging, and its effect on the penis, has nothing to do with masculinity—not unless *you* make that bridge. You can't stop your partner from questioning his own masculinity if he is determined to do so. I know that. But you can stop yourself from adding fuel to that fire. If anything can help a man disassemble the "masculinity = performance ability" equation, it is *your* refusal to give it any credibility.

Note also that some of the most "unreal" (as in superficial, phony, dishonest, narcissistic, etc.) men are perfect performers with flawless erections. Yet the sex, as you may know from your own experience, is awful.

THE ATTITUDE: *"If He Can't Make Love to Me the Way He Used to, It Means He Doesn't Love Me"*

THE REALITY: Men's sexual changes after 50 have *nothing* to do with love, and *everything* to do with changes in blood circulation, loss of critical muscle tone, different requirements for stimulation, a shift in sensitivity and a need for more rest. To make a long story short, it's his natural aging process. Now that you understand the workings of a temperamental penis, aren't you ready to stop personalizing *his* changes? Maybe, with a few new ideas and a little bit of practice, your lovemaking will become *better* than it ever was. It easily can. But it's not going to happen if you're beating yourself up and withdrawing. And it's not going to happen if you start beating *him* up, either.

THE ATTITUDE: *"I Can Judge How Much My Partner Loves Me by the Strength of His Erection"*

THE REALITY: Your partner may love you to death, but the strength of his erection is likely to change as he ages. It's not his love that is changing—his love may be stronger than ever—the hydraulic machine is just showing its years. Love and hardness are not one and the same thing.

THE ATTITUDE: *"I Can Judge How Much My Partner Loves Me by the Force of His Ejaculation"*

THE REALITY: The force of a man's ejaculation depends far more on the strength of his PC muscle than on the strength of his loving heart. This muscle naturally loses its strength and tone over time unless a man is actively exercising it. This is one of the reasons why I have incorporated a simple but powerful PC program into this book.

The volume of semen is also likely to decrease with age, and this, too, has nothing to do with love. It has to do with a slowing down in semen production in the testicles, enlargement of the prostate and the reabsorption of semen from the urethral bulb back into the testicles. Getting on a regular ejaculation schedule can actually increase the volume of semen by regularly clearing out the prostate. This is a very healthy habit for any man over 50.

THE ATTITUDE: *"Men Are Always Ready to Have Sex—If They're Not Ready, Something Is Wrong"*

THE REALITY: Every man has a "receptivity cycle"—there are times when his body is more responsive, and times when it is less responsive. This becomes more and more pronounced as a man ages, and is also influenced by emotional factors, the quality of his sleep and so on. This is one reason why a man is not *always* ready to have sex. And there is another reason . . .

After orgasm and ejaculation, men go through a rest-and-recovery phase referred to as the *refractory period* (we will discuss this in detail in chapter 8). As men age, the duration of this physiological time-out generally increases, and after 50 this becomes more obvious. As noted earlier, what may have taken thirty minutes just a few years ago (and thirty seconds thirty years ago) now may take a while longer. This does not mean your partner is losing interest in sex, it just means he needs more physiological down time.

He may not act sexual during this resting phase, but this should not be misinterpreted as a loss of interest or a problem.

Women discover that their willingness to be more *playful* and less intensely sexual during this down time actually encourages a man to be more open to contact. A playful, accepting attitude also encourages a man to reconnect with his returning sexual impulses, often leading to renewed sexual activity— even if it is not intercourse. It is the *demand* for sex, or the perceived demand, that makes so many men fearful and unwilling to be at all sexual unless they know they can deliver.

THE ATTITUDE: *"If My Partner Can't Get an Erection Spontaneously, Something Is Wrong"*

THE REALITY: There are many men who have experienced years of effortless, spontaneous erections— erections that happen in the absence of any direct physical stimulation—before their body starts to change. Their partners get used to this automatic response—often forming stereotypical notions such as, "All he needs is a good breeze to get him hard." But it is completely unrealistic for any woman to expect a man to be able to have spontaneous erections throughout the course of his entire life. It is simply naive to believe that is the only way the penis functions. And it is destructive to conclude that something is wrong if erections no longer appear spontaneously. Nothing is "wrong." Something is *different*—the hydraulic system is showing its years. But your partner probably has *decades* of beautiful erections still in him. He just may need a little bit of assistance from now on.

THE ATTITUDE: *"My Partner Shouldn't Need My Help to Get and Keep His Erection"*

THE REALITY: Many women are not used to being active partners in the bedroom. Maybe they'll caress their partner for a few minutes, or perform a little bit of oral sex if they're in the mood, but then they rely on the man to take charge, and they rely on his penis to function effectively. They don't believe they need to get involved in the erection process, and they remain quite unschooled in the art of genital stimulation. I call this passive approach to sex "the do-me's" (as in, "I'm going to lie back and you can do me").

A woman who has always relied on her partner's spontaneous erections and active role, and who is unschooled in the arts of genital stimulation, is going to need a quick education. But the first class she needs to attend is an attitude adjustment class—Loving New Attitudes 101. It is destructive to demand that the penis does its own work. *Erections are an exercise in partnership*, and this becomes more and more critical as a man ages.

THE ATTITUDE: *"If My Partner Loses His Erection When We Are Having Sex, It Means I Turned Him Off"*

THE REALITY: As men age, the strength of a man's erection tends to be less consistent. Just because a penis is fully erect when intercourse begins (a 10 on a 1–10 scale), it doesn't mean it will *stay* completely erect through orgasm. The degree of hardness may vary—it could, for example, vary between a 6 and a 10—particularly if intercourse is prolonged. And guess what? It probably has nothing to do with you. Body movements become more critical, body positioning becomes more critical (remember what you've learned about circulation), the intensity of the stimulation becomes more critical and stressors (job pressure, ringing telephones, etc.) have more of an impact.

Too many women jump to the conclusion that the slightest change means something awful has happened. Instead of riding the wave of change, they panic and start looking for problems. Some start asking, "What's wrong? What's wrong?" Some will say, "I guess you're not into it." And some will just withdraw. None of this is constructive or appropriate.

THE ATTITUDE: *"If My Partner Has to Stimulate Himself to Get an Erection or an Orgasm, There Is Something Wrong with Me"*

THE REALITY: As a man gets older, his needs for stimulation tend to get far more specific. Gone are the days when anything and everything felt perfect. If your partner has started to get more "hands-on" during lovemaking to get an erection or help bring himself to orgasm, it usually reflects these more specific needs. He knows what he needs, and he's probably just trying to make it *easier* for you, not to make you feel bad. This is a growth opportunity—an opportunity for you to express an interest in learning more about what makes him feel good. Take advantage of it. And allow him to continue his participation—if that is the best solution—without making him feel judged.

THE ATTITUDE: *"If My Partner Can't Have an Orgasm—or a Strong Orgasm—It's Because the Sex Doesn't Feel Good"*

THE REALITY: Many men have an increasingly difficult time reaching orgasm as they age because their need for stimulation becomes very specific, and they cannot always meet that need through intercourse. The sex feels good—it just doesn't provide the necessary build-up for orgasm. This is why it becomes very important for a woman to relearn, with the honest participation of her partner, manual and oral stimulation techniques.

The intensity of a man's orgasm often diminishes with age, due at least in part to lack of strength in the

PC muscle. As I have said before, the PC muscle—like every other muscle in the body—degenerates gradually over the years. The sex may still feel wonderful. It may feel better than ever, since many men experience heightened sensitivity as they get older. But orgasm itself may be problematic because the muscle is not strong enough to effectively spasm. We'll discuss orgasm more in the next chapter, but note that the PC exercises in chapter 5 are the best remedy for this diminished intensity problem.

THE ATTITUDE: *"If My Partner Can't Get an Erection, It's Because He's Not Trying Hard Enough"*

THE REALITY: If your partner can't get an erection, it's probably because he's trying *too* hard. He may be squeezing muscles that cut off the flow of blood to the penis, or he may be squeezing his brain—making unreasonable internal demands—and cutting off the erection process completely. Self-imposed sexual pressure does not facilitate the erection process; it completely sabotages the process. And the same goes for partner-imposed pressure. A man's body needs to be relaxed and open to pleasurable stimulation, and his mind needs to be *more* relaxed and *more* open. Sexual demands—whether they are his or yours—never lead to a positive result.

THE ATTITUDE: *"If My Partner Can't Get an Erection, He's Doing It on Purpose to Withhold Sex from Me"*

THE REALITY: Before you play amateur therapist and jump to destructive conclusions, try to consider some of the more likely possibilities. As you should be starting to understand, there are so many things that can interfere with the erection process: sexual pressure (his own pressure, your pressure), stress, circulation, stimulation, sleep, timing. Maybe you feel punished by your partner's performance problems, but that doesn't mean he's *trying* to punish you. If he can't get an erection, he's probably feeling a lot worse than you are. And if you can't sort this out together, as a couple, seeking professional couples' counseling would be a prudent investment.

THE ATTITUDE: *"If My Partner Is Going to Lose His Erection in the Middle of Having Sex, I'd Rather Not Have Sex at All"*

THE REALITY: As a man ages, it may become more difficult for him to maintain a firm erection for an extended period of time. To accommodate this, some women will ask for more foreplay, and let themselves have an orgasm *before* intercourse begins. Then they feel more free to enjoy the "ups and downs" of their partner's performance. Other women will incorporate

the use of intense manual stimulation (or, perhaps
even better, a vibrator) during intercourse to facilitate
orgasm in a shorter window of time. Still others will
learn intercourse techniques that minimize a woman's
need for prolonged penetration while taking nothing
away from the experience of orgasm. (I wrote about
this extensively in *Discover Your Sensual Potential,*
and will include a few interesting examples later in
this book). You have *many* choices. The worst, most
punitive, most destructive choice is not having sex at
all. It only puts more pressure on your partner, creating *more* problems, and it builds walls that are hard
to bring down.

THE ATTITUDE: *"If My Partner Wants to Make
Love, He'll Let Me Know"*

THE REALITY: When a man starts to lose his sexual
confidence, he may become less capable of acting on
his sexual impulses. The desire may be there, but the
fear of being less than perfect creates a barrier he cannot always overcome. Men may lose their playful
spontaneity and some of their aggressiveness. And
this may give the appearance of less interest.

Your partner will want to make love far more often
if he feels a sense of acceptance and playfulness on
your part. If he thinks he has to be perfect to be
acceptable, he may keep many of his sexual impulses
to himself.

THE ATTITUDE: *"If We're Doing Something That Doesn't Feel Good, My Partner Will Let Me Know"*

THE REALITY: Everyone has a hard time introducing new information into a sexual relationship—particularly a long-standing sexual relationship. Most people—both men and women—are just too afraid of rocking the boat. They're afraid of creating hurt feelings, they're afraid of raising unnecessary suspicions, they're afraid of retaliation (e.g., "Well, since we're on the subject, I've got a list of things . . ."). It's like telling someone after twenty years that you are no longer in love with their prize lasagna dinner. It's easier to just keep quiet and keep eating. Easier, but not very gratifying.

One of the hardest adjustments that getting older brings to the bedroom is the reality that many things that were perfectly fine for years and years are no longer satisfactory. We can make believe that nothing has changed. Or we can be courageous, and open a loving dialogue.

THE ATTITUDE: *"Sexual Intercourse Is the Only 'Real' Sex—If Foreplay Doesn't Lead to Intercourse, What's the Point?"*

THE REALITY: Many women still subscribe to this very convoluted definition of sexual intimacy. This is like saying to your partner, "If you can't get it up, I'm not interested." Your sex life is bound to deteriorate under this kind of pressure. For a man, aging typically leads to less than perfect performance. Sooner or later, he's going to have a bad day. Or a bad week. Or a bad year. That's *natural*. But the emotional pressure from a rigid notion such as this is unnatural—it creates a problem where there was no problem, and it turns molehills into mountains.

Intercourse is only one kind of sexual interaction. Part of creating a new world of lovemaking with a 50-plus partner is incorporating oral sex, sexual massage and other forms of love play into your repertoire. Sometimes these things are a prelude to intercourse, but other times they *are* the main course.

THE ATTITUDE: *"If a Guy Can't Get It Up, He's Got a Problem I Can't Fix"*

THE SEXUAL REALITY: Maybe you *can't* "fix" your partner's penis so that it becomes the perfect performer. But some attitude fixing can bring dramatic results. First, stop thinking of it as a *problem*. Your negativity only makes things worse. And abusive, berating language practically *guarantees* performance problems.

Second, learn more about what feels good to your partner right now, and what doesn't feel that good. His body sensitivity has probably changed. You need to learn about those changes. Perhaps a loving touch from you is enough to bring his erection to life, but he's been afraid to ask for that because it is not a part of your standard sexual repertoire.

Third, understand that your role is always crucial—you are never less than 50 percent of his pleasure. It's time to accept that responsibility.

THE ATTITUDE: *"If My Partner's Interest in Sex Is Waning, It's Because of Me"*

THE SEXUAL REALITY: If your partner's interest in sex is waning, it is probably because he is confused by the way his body is changing. He may feel tentative about his ability to perform, fearful of disappointing you and worried about what's in store for the future. Remember, also, that hormonal changes will be affecting his overall level of desire. Once again, this isn't about *you*—it's about being over 50. If you want to *do* something to encourage his interest, don't go the peekaboo bra route just yet. Start with some reassuring words that make your love and commitment clear.

You've Got a New Attitude

Sexual attitudes are not carved in stone. They can change with education and motivation, and I'm hoping you've been getting a healthy dose of both. **Most women don't realize how much power they wield in their relationships, and how sensitive their partners**

are to their judgments. Everything you think, say and do has an impact on your partner's sexuality. Everything. You can make him feel good about himself and you can make him feel bad about himself. You can ease his anxieties or you can add to his anxieties. You can enhance his performance abilities or you can sabotage those abilities. You are powerful.

So think about the messages you have been sending your partner. Think about your words. Your behavior. Your touch. Your body language. Are you consistently sending messages of love, acceptance, openness and enthusiasm? Or do your messages sometimes convey confusion, closed-mindedness, frustration, blame, judgment, disappointment, demand, anger or self-flagellation? Even the most subtle things—a sigh, a shrug, a frown, a turn of the head—send strong signals to a sensitive partner who is, perhaps for the very first time, concerned about the impact of his changing sexuality. You have the power to bring out the best in your man, and the time to start is now.

7

Experimenting with Arousal

How do you know when your partner is aroused? Is his erection the only clear sign you know to interpret? This can be very confusing when his penis no longer responds as quickly and efficiently as it used to. As a man passes the fifty-year marker in his life, his erection is no longer the best barometer of his experience of arousal, or pleasure or *anything*. He can be excited, but not erect. He can be erect, but not terribly excited. He can have an orgasm without an erection. He can have an erection, but fail to have an orgasm. His erection can go up and down while his desire remains constant. His desire can go up and down while his erection remains constant. It's all terribly confusing.

Making love to a man over 50 means becoming an expert in his arousal. And that means paying more attention to your partner's sexual nuances than you ever have before and letting this new information in. You need to have the ability to micromanage his arousal—to take him exactly where he needs to go. But you can't do that if you're still in the automatic pilot mode. Remember, sex after 50 is not business as usual. Yet it can be new, and different, and so much better! So get excited about the possibilities, then get back to work.

Learning to Be Playful

Your sexual relationship cannot flourish if it is not growing in fertile soil. And love is not enough. Sexual demands inhibit sexual growth, yet *most* **acts of sexual intimacy have built-in demands,** either subtle or obvious. There is the demand for an erection. The demand for mutual satisfaction. The demand for penetration. The demand for orgasm. The demand for ejaculation. It's not as though you are turning to your partner and saying, "I demand penetration!" (At least, I hope you're not.) And it's not as though he's turning to you and saying, "I demand you bring me to orgasm!" (At least, I hope he's not.) But the very act of engaging in sex engages these voices in our heads. And yes, sometimes they even pop out of our mouths.

This is where *non-demand sexual play* comes in. Non-demand sexual play is the sex therapist's best friend, and you are going to make it your best friend. It is a healing tool, it is a loving tool and it is a growth tool.

- *Non-demand sexual play means there are no goals.* Orgasm is not the goal. Erection is not the goal. Intercourse is not the goal. Anything *can* happen, but play must be free and spontaneous.

- *Non-demand sexual play means there are no judgments.* There are no rights and wrongs. There is only "that feels good" and "that doesn't feel as good."

- *Non-demand sexual play means being open to trying new things.* Not wild, edge-of-the-envelope stuff, but things that may be new for *you.*

When was the last time you and your partner did anything that remotely resembled non-demand sexual play? When was the last time you kissed just for the fun of it, or massaged each other without having sex as the goal, or played with each other's genitals just for the pleasure of exploration and intimate contact? These are things that most couples just don't do, yet they are the very things you need to be doing if you want to learn about the ways your partner is changing, and let him learn about the ways *you* are changing.

Starting Slow, Starting Safe

It is time for you to learn about the pleasures of sensate focus touching, and to introduce these same pleasures to the man you love. Sensate focus touching is not a sex act, it is a form of non-demand sexual play that ignites the senses and educates the body.

Here are the rules:

RULE 1: Pay attention to *exactly* where you are touching, or where you are being touched. Stay as focused as possible.

RULE 2: Stay in the here and now. Try to let go of anything that is not happening at this very moment in the room with your partner. Leave daily concerns like bills, work and family outside the door.

RULE 3: No pressure. Don't pressure yourself, don't pressure your partner and don't let your partner pressure you. The only goal is to touch and be touched for the experience of pleasure.

RULE 4: Touch for your own pleasure, *not* your partner's pleasure. Don't do anything that doesn't feel good to *you*.

RULE 5: GO SLOW.

The best way to get comfortable with the concept of sensate focus touching is to begin with a loving, simple facial exercise. . . .

Exercise 1: Facial Familiarity

Begin by telling your partner you wish to spend five loving minutes exploring the contours of his face with your hands. It is nice to have very soft, sensual music playing in the background. Now close your eyes, and ask him to close his eyes. Slowly, using just the tips of your fingers, rest both hands lightly on your partner's face and explore the surfaces. Imagine that he is a stranger you have just met. What does the face of this stranger feel like? What might he look like? What areas are rough and what areas are smooth? What areas are warm and what areas are cool? Where is there tension? Where is there openness? What does it feel like as he starts to smile? You have looked at your partner's face thousands of times—what can you feel about his face that you have never really noticed before?

After five minutes, give your partner the chance to explore *your* face.

This next sensate focus exercise feels best in a room lit with soft candlelight. Soft, sensual music is also recommended.

Exercise 2: Eye to Eye

Once again you are going to explore your partner's face with your fingertips for a full five minutes. But this time your eyes and his eyes should be open, and you want to maintain sincere eye contact the entire time. Let your fingers do the feeling as your eyes do the holding.

After five minutes, let your lips show your pleasure by exploring his face with soft kisses. Pay attention to the subtle tastes of his beard, his scalp, his chin, his lips and so on. Do not engage in deep kissing, and maintain eye contact wherever possible.

After a few more minutes, change roles and give your partner the opportunity to have the same experience of you.

Waking the Body

You are now ready to learn the full body caress—a slow, gentle fingertip exploration of the body. This exercise should be done in a quiet room with a comfortable bed (thick towels or blankets on the floor are also acceptable)—a room that is free from distractions. Lock the door to ensure that no one can enter suddenly. You will need massage oil, cream, K-Y jelly or some other lubricant. Be sure to use a lubricant that does not irritate the genitals (for women, K-Y is usually the safest choice). Have a clean towel handy. Keep the lights low, or use two or three slow-burning candles.

Exercise 3: The Body Touch

Ask your partner to remove his clothes, lie on his back and get very comfortable. Cover his groin with a large towel (don't taunt him with a teeny washcloth he will be tempted to brush aside). Encourage him to take several deep breaths, exhaling to a count of five—deep breath in, slow breath out, one–two–three–four–five. Now ask him to close his eyes. In this exercise, your partner has a completely *passive* role. He is not supposed to *do* anything but enjoy the experience.

You, on the other hand, will be playing the *active* role. You're supposed to be enjoying the experience, too, but you are also in complete control.

Starting at his neck, use your fingers to explore the many surfaces of his body, *excluding* his genitals. Keep your caresses slow and deliberate. Use lots of lubrication to ensure that your motion is smooth. Move to his shoulder blades, his shoulders, his arms, his hands, his fingertips. Work your way back up his arms to his chest, then down his chest to his stomach. Go slow, slow, slow. Pay careful attention to what each part of his body feels like and looks like. Absorb yourself in those sensations, trying to create a memory in your hands and in your eyes.

All your partner needs to do is lie still, remain completely relaxed and appreciate your touch. He is not supposed to reciprocate in any way. And his eyes should remain closed. The only time he should talk is if something is making him uncomfortable. If your partner is tensing up, tap that muscle gently as a signal to him that he needs to relax it. You should make this signal clear to him before you begin.

Immerse yourself in the touch, and the way it feels to touch each part of him. If you get distracted or your mind starts to wander, don't suddenly stop. Instead, slowly bring yourself back to a place of intense concentration—refocus your mind on the caress. It doesn't matter how many times your mind strays. All that matters is that you recognize the shift and bring your mind back to the exercise. If you find yourself getting bored or mechanical, it usually means your movements are rushed. Cut your speed in half and try harder to stay in the moment.

From the stomach, continue down the sides of his body to his hips. Be certain to avoid contact with his groin right now. You'll have ample opportunity for that later. Work slowly down his thighs to his knees, to his calves, to his ankles, to his feet, to his toes. Continue using plenty of lubrication. Once you have reached his toes, you may want to change direction and retrace your steps all the way back to his neck.

You should spend between twenty and forty minutes with this exercise. The most important thing is that it cannot be rushed. When you have finished the caress, your partner may want to return the favor. That's fine, but he shouldn't feel that he *has* to reciprocate. The caress is your gift to him.

Your next gift to your partner is the genital caress. You don't want to perform this the same day as the full-body caress—wait at least a day or two. Even better, wait a week, to let his anticipation build. Once again, you will want to be in a quiet room with a comfortable bed and low light. You will need plenty of lubrication and a clean towel.

Exercise 4: The Genital Touch

Ask your partner to remove his clothes, lie on his back and get very comfortable. Cover his groin with a clean towel. Encourage him to take a series of slow, deep breaths, following each one with a long (five-second count) exhale. Ask him to close his eyes and do nothing but enjoy the pleasure of your touch. His role in this exercise is completely passive.

Starting at his chest, use your fingers to begin exploring the surfaces of his body. Use lots of lubrication. Move from his chest, to his stomach, to his thighs. From his thighs, slowly approach his genital area, pushing the towel away bit by bit as your hands move closer. First, let your fingers *gently* explore his scrotum, holding the testicles in your fingertips. Let your fingers wander behind the scrotum to the area where you can feel his PC muscle. Work back around his thighs to his pubic mound, then slowly toward the penis.

Once you begin to caress the penis, do *not* change to a masturbation stroke. This is a sensate focus exploration with the fingertips, not a masturbation exercise. Your goal is not to stimulate him, it is to become intimate with the pleasurable sensations of gently caressing his genitals. He may indeed be *very* stimulated, but you are not supposed to *do* something about that—you are only to continue your soft caress.

Travel up and down the penis, exploring the head, the shaft and the area at the base. If his penis is becoming erect (which is not the goal and not necessary), travel up and down the ridge on the underside of the penis, around the front, way up to the tip and then back down to the scrotum. Travel behind the scrotum through the area between his anus and his testicles.

Enjoy the sensations and stay focused in the here and now. Notice the areas where he seems particularly sensitive. Watch his breathing. Feel his heartbeat. Watch for tension in his muscles. Enjoy the ebb and flow of his excitement. Don't rush. The emphasis is on sensuality, not sexuality. The pleasure comes from having him in your hands and exploring every bit of that. His arousal will be evident from the quality of his breathing, the flush of his skin, the sounds that he makes, the changes in his pulse and the response of his penis.

Continue this genital caress for no less than twenty minutes. Remember to signal your partner to relax if you sense tension in the muscles of his body, particularly his thigh muscles, stomach muscles and buttock muscles. When you are done, give your partner the opportunity to perform a reciprocal genital massage, if that is something you would enjoy.

Erection and arousal are two separate processes, but each can certainly influence the other. And *you* can influence *both*. In the next exercise, you are going to clearly see the direct impact of improved circulation on the erection process. This exercise is an important learning tool, but it is also an exercise that many women choose to incorporate into their regular lovemaking because it can make such a difference in the strength of their partner's erections *and* arousal.

Exercise 5: The Hub

Begin this exercise as if you were beginning the full body caress (Exercise 3). But this time, your strokes are going to be firmer—more like a good massage stroke than a light caress. You are going to need lots of lubrication for this. Don't be afraid to apply more continually. Your partner's eyes need to remain closed, and he needs to remain passive during the entire exercise. His only job is to enjoy the sensations you are providing.

Take the towel away from your partner's groin so that his penis and testicles are unencumbered, and completely visible to you. Imagine now that your partner's groin is the hub of a wheel, and his legs and his upper torso are the spokes. What you are going to do in this exercise is massage these three spokes, one at a time, with your massage strokes moving in only one direction: *toward* the groin.

Start with his left thigh. Using two hands, work the skin and muscle of his leg with sensual but firm (not painful, please!) strokes. Imagine that you are trying to move the blood from his leg toward his groin. After a few minutes, switch to his other leg. After a few more minutes, move to his stomach muscles and work your way down toward the pubic mound.

You do not want to massage the groin directly, and you do not want to touch his genitals. You just want to work the thighs, the hips, the stomach and the pubic mound and *watch* the effect this has on his erection. You are literally using your hands to enhance the flow of blood to his penis and encourage the filling process we talked about in chapter 4. Continue this exercise for at least fifteen minutes. Then proceed to the next exercise.

Aroused and Aware

How well does your partner know the strength of his own arousal? How well do *you* think you know his levels of arousal? In this next exercise, you will both see how much there is to learn about erections and male arousal. To facilitate this exercise, it helps to have in your mind a partner "arousal scale" you can use as a reference. Imagine a 1-to-10 scale where 10 is a fully aroused partner in the throes of orgasm, and 1 is a completely unaroused partner with no obvious signs of excitement. At levels 3 and 4 you can see the stirrings of your partner's sexual interest by the appearance of some tension in his muscles, the change in his breathing, a rising pulse and probably some swelling of his penis. At 5, the halfway point, you definitely have his attention, and it would be unkind to quit. By level 7 or 8, the breathing and the tension in his muscles are far more intense, his penis may be throbbing, and it would be really unpleasant to suddenly stop—hopefully, unpleasant for both of you.

Note that these arousal levels are not "hardness of the penis" levels. They are about your partner's experience of pleasure and excitement, not the behavior of his penis.

Exercise 6: Where Am I?

Approach this exercise as though you were playing a game called "How excited are you now?" Your partner will need to understand the basic "arousal scale" before you begin. Don't make it too complicated. If he understands a 1 and a 10, he'll probably be able to figure out the rest.

The game starts with your partner closing his eyes. It may be fun for him to use a blindfold, if he prefers that. Once again, your partner has a completely passive role—his only job is to enjoy the exercise. The object of this exercise is to use your caressing and massaging techniques to create different levels of arousal in your partner. As

you practice the techniques you have been learning, periodically stop what you are doing for a
moment and ask, "How excited are you now?"

How does his answer to your question—what
he tells you *he* is feeling—correspond to what *you*
are seeing, feeling and imagining? How rapidly is
he breathing? Are his muscles tense? What noises
does he make? Does his skin color change? Is he
starting to perspire? Is his pulse quickening? How
does his arousal level compare to the strength of
his erection? Make sure your partner doesn't
open his eyes—you don't want the sight of his
own erection, or lack of erection, to confuse him.

Continue practicing your techniques, stopping
every two or three minutes to ask, "How excited
are you?" Make extensive mental notes from his
answers. Note his breathing, his coloring, his
pulse, his sounds, his perspiration and, of course,
his penis. Does he say he feels fully aroused, but
his erection is barely at level 5? That's an interesting piece of information for both of you. Does he
say he's not feeling that aroused yet, yet his erection tells an impressively different story? That's
an interesting piece of information, too. Look for
the signs that *really* tell the story. BUT MOST
IMPORTANT: Note what he responds to most
powerfully from *you*. Does he like the touches
you think he likes? Does the speed of your touch
make a difference? Does the strength of your

touch make a difference? Does the rhythm of your touch make a difference? Do the areas you touch make a difference? Do certain things that you pay little attention to make a big difference to him? This is vital information. Spend at least twenty minutes practicing your arousal techniques this way and taking in feedback from your partner.

The object of this arousal exercise is not to judge your partner's perceptions. The object is to give both of you a clearer picture of how he feels throughout his arousal process and how much power you have to make a difference in that process. Through this exercise you will learn which kinds of caressing and massaging techniques *feel* best to your partner, and which have the greatest impact on his erection process. The techniques that *feel* best may not necessarily be the ones that produce the most visible results. Your partner may prefer *sensual* techniques that don't necessarily foster a full erection, or he may prefer more direct stimulation techniques that directly translate into hardness. Every man is different, and there are no bad choices. The important thing is to *know* his choices so you can take some of the guesswork out of your lovemaking. Be open to new information. **Even if you have been making love to your partner for twenty or thirty years, there is always something new to learn about the specifics of his arousal.**

From Arousal to Penetration

It is time to put it all together—the exercises, the techniques and the information you have acquired thus far—and build your first bridge from arousal to lovemaking. You have been very loving and very patient—it is time for you to reap a few rewards for that love and patience.

Exercise 7: Penetration Technique

This exercise can continue from Exercise 5 or Exercise 6. Once again, your partner has a completely passive role. His eyes must remain closed. He cannot move during the exercise (not his hands, not his legs, not his hips). You are the only one who will be moving.

If you have been wearing clothing for the previous exercise, you need to remove that clothing now. Begin practicing the techniques you have learned to increase your partner's level of arousal. In addition, use the technique of moving blood to his groin to encourage his erection. In this exercise, you can also stimulate his penis more aggressively with your hands, as described in chapter 4.

Straddle your partner's body and continue your arousing massage. Try not to rest your weight on his legs, because this will cut off the necessary circulation. Make sure his penis is well lubricated. As your partner's penis becomes firm (by firm, I mean about a 5 or 6 on a 1-to-10 hardness scale), hold his penis in your hand and use it to gently caress your clitoris and the lips of your vagina. Orgasm is not your goal—not for either one of you. Just enjoy the sensations of his penis rubbing your genitals.

If his erection is strengthening, stop the stimulation for a minute or two, allowing his erection to subside. Now slowly start working with your stimulation technique and special blood flow technique, *using lots of lubrication*. Again, hold his penis and use it to rub up and down on your genital area. When his erection is firm enough to enter you (say a 7 or 8 on a 1-to-10 hardness scale—it doesn't need to be rock-hard), let the head of his penis slip into your vagina. Gently *push* it in if it's not quite hard enough to enter easily. You'll need to be generous with that lubrication.

Take his penis back out and continue your slow massage. After a minute or two, insert it again and move up and down on his penis for two or three strokes. Remove it from your vagina and let his erection subside again. After a brief rest, begin your blood flow massage and other stimulation techniques. As his penis stiffens, use it to once again massage the lips of your vagina. Slip the head of the penis inside you for two or three strokes, and remove it again.

Continue this for several more rounds: massage, rub, insert, withdraw. Rest and repeat. If you want to finish this exercise by masturbating your partner to orgasm, that's fine. If he has an orgasm during the exercise, that's fine, too (PLEASE EXERCISE THE PRECAUTIONS YOU *ALWAYS* EXERCISE WHEN YOU HAVE SEX WITH YOUR PARTNER). If *you* have an orgasm, that's great. But remember that orgasm is *not* the goal of this exercise—not for anyone.

Conquering Penetration Anxiety

This penetration exercise is not just for arousal education. It will help diminish your partner's experience of "penetration anxiety"—a common phenomenon among men over 50. As the penis becomes less dependable, men begin to have concerns about their ability to penetrate their partner's vagina: "Will my penis be hard enough?" "Will I be able to get in?" "If my penis falls out during thrusting, will I be able to get *back* in?" These worries make many men timid, and sometimes even afraid of having intercourse unless they feel absolutely perfect. The penetration exercise you just learned gets men comfortable experiencing penetration with a less-than-perfect erection. They see that penetration is still possible. They see that it still gives you pleasure. They see that their erections can ebb and flow without being a problem. And all of this is a powerful confidence-builder. As you will see, **confidence-builders are erection-builders**.

Opening More Doors: A Few Practical Suggestions

If you are going to make the transition from being a couple who has sex to being a sexual couple, it is crucial that you create a mood of openness and acceptance at all times. If sex is something you will only have on a Saturday night at ten o'clock, both you and your partner have slowly trained yourselves to suppress any sexual impulses that are not in sync with that schedule. But over time, that suppression tends to shut down the system completely. You can't restrict lovemaking to a tiny window in your life and expect it to flourish in that minuscule space.

It's time to open some doors—doors that have probably been closed for a very long time. Your partner needs to know that his sexuality is *always* welcome. This doesn't mean that you are going to have sex every single time he has an erection; it just means that you are going to make it clear to him that you always *appreciate* his sexual impulses. Always. They are exciting to you. They are flattering to you. And you want to know more about them. You are not promising action. You are only conveying sincere interest. His fly may need to stay zipped, but you want his mind and body to open. And you want your mind and body to be equally open. The following suggestions will help you show your newfound interest and enthusiasm in your partner's arousal . . .

New Sleeping Habits: Sleep nude on your side so that you are pressed up against your partner's penis in the morning. Whether or not it is erect, and whether or not you want to have sex, *always* make it clear to him that you enjoy feeling him.

A Morning Massage: Gently massage your partner's penis in the morning before both of you get out of bed. Some women will be able to do this without even waking their partner. Practice the circulation-enhancing pubic mound massage, too. Do this as a feel-good massage, not as a necessary precursor to intercourse.

The Love Handle: Periodically let your partner know how aware you are of his sexuality by resting your hand firmly on his penis (clothed or unclothed) and offering him positive reinforcement. You may want to tell him something like, "I love holding you" or "I love the way that looks" or "I love the way that feels in my hand" or "That's so nice." Or you may just want to smile. Don't turn it into a lovemaking session—just make it a clear, unapologetic gesture of appreciation. Keep it private, and keep it safe (not while he's driving, please!).

Nap Time: Has your partner taken to falling asleep early in the evening as he watches television or reads? That's a wonderful time to snuggle up to him and practice your caressing and massage skills. Don't try to startle him (and don't wake him if he needs the rest)—keep it gentle and loving. Do it just for the pleasure.

All of these suggestions accomplish the same thing: They tell your partner that his sexuality is always *welcome*. You are not promising sex—you are showing interest, enthusiasm and acceptance. All of the above suggestions are to be practiced with no demands and no pressure to perform. **Touch him because you enjoy touching him, and because this is something you always want him to know.**

8

Orgasm, Ejaculation and Love After 50

I am often asked what I consider to be the single greatest physiological *roadblock to male sexual potency after 50*. And my answer is going to surprise you. It isn't hormones. It isn't blood circulation. It isn't fatigue. It isn't those extra pounds. It isn't lack of exercise. And it isn't lack of practice. From my extensive experience, it has become crystal-clear to me that men start to have problems with lovemaking after they turn 50 because *they are not highly orgasmic*. Men are not highly orgasmic *before* they turn 50. And they are even *less* orgasmic after 50. One of the most important secrets to making love to a man over 50 is helping him become truly, fully orgasmic. Now, before I am accused of heresy, I had better explain what I have just said.

Most Men Under 50 Are Not Highly Orgasmic

The typical male orgasm is not an experience most women would envy. I know this looks as if I'm male-bashing, but I'm really stating what is clear and obvious to any professional sex therapist. This doesn't mean that men don't have orgasms, it doesn't mean that they can't have lots of orgasms and it doesn't mean that they don't *like* their orgasms. What it means is that men don't tend to have the glorious, full-body orgasms that so many women experience on a regular basis.

Most men learn at a very early age to focus on the simple release phase of sex—that is, their ejaculation. Masturbation tends to be very rushed and goal-oriented, fueled, no doubt, by some element of shame, embarrassment or awkwardness. The result is a cut-to-the-chase approach to sex that is efficient and sufficiently gratifying. And if you're fifteen years old, it's usually good enough.

As men begin to have sex partners, they are even *less* motivated to immerse themselves in their own orgasmic potential. As I said in chapter 1, these men are on a mission to numb themselves and delay their orgasm for the sake of their partners. They don't want to get *too* excited. Ejaculation is one of the few pleasures men do ultimately allow themselves, but even this has complications, since there are often concerns about unwanted pregnancy. Most men under 50 don't know how to tap into the larger group of exquisite sensations that can be summoned from the body through excitement, orgasm and ejaculation. The dramatic changes in heart rate and breathing, the tensing and untensing of various muscles, the glorious sensitization of the skin, the build-up of energy and anticipation—*most* of this is lost on the typical male.

The upshot is that **the typical male orgasm lacks power**. Most men under 50 experience their orgasm as a very localized phenomenon—a groin-centered phenomenon. It's a good sneeze-like sensation. Maybe even a great sneeze-like sensation. But it's just a sneeze. You don't see too many men biting their pillows, or becoming teary-eyed from the pure bliss of it. You don't hear them shouting at the top of their lungs and waking the neighbors. They enjoy the release, but they are missing a lot.

If there is any "envy complex" Freud should have noticed and explored, it is the envy men must experience as they watch their female partners being consumed by the experience of orgasm. Who wouldn't want some of that action?

The interesting thing is that men and women aren't as different as they appear to be. Certainly not as far as orgasm is concerned. Like women, men have the *potential* to summon extraordinary sensations from throughout the body and flood themselves with their own orgasmic power. But this has to be *learned*. It's just that very few men under the age of 50 have the motivation to learn—they don't want to become less ejaculation-centered and retrain their body to follow a different path. They don't even think about it.

After the age of 50, however, they start thinking. As the intensity of ejaculation release diminishes—as it does in so many men after the age of 50—the experience of orgasm also diminishes. Men lose the sense of power and virility that a strong ejaculation brings, and they lose the heady rush. The big sneeze becomes a big snooze. And when that happens, you have a partner who is ripe for experiencing something new.

Understanding the Difference Between Ejaculation and Orgasm

Am I confusing you because I talk about male orgasm and ejaculation as though they were not one and the same thing? After all, isn't ejaculation *the* main ingredient in a man's orgasm? Well . . . yes, and no. And this statement is as perplexing for men as it is for women.

Here is a very basic piece of physiological information that the majority of *men* don't even know: Ejaculation and male orgasm are two separate and distinct physiological processes that typically occur as one for the average male. While most men understandably *equate* orgasm with ejaculation, and could not imagine one without the other, the male orgasm does not have to include an ejaculation to be a bona fide orgasm. In fact, some men work very hard to have ejaculation-free orgasms because it enables them to have *additional* orgasms without losing their erection. We'll talk more about this later.

Here's something else you should know: A man can ejaculate without ever having an orgasm. This happens to many men when they are asleep (it is the so-called "nocturnal emission"), and it happens to some men who are wide awake, particularly as they get older and their orgasm reflex loses its punch.

What Is Ejaculation?

An ejaculation is the expulsion of semen out of the opening in the urethra at the tip of the penis. As I discussed in the brief anatomy lesson in chapter 4, this happens when the urethral bulb spasms and the PC muscle contracts. The combination of spasms and contractions is a potent force—particularly when the PC muscle is strong and the prostate is healthy—and out goes the semen into a brave new world.

So . . . What Is Orgasm?

Orgasm is something else entirely. Yes, orgasm *can* trigger the ejaculation. But there is so much more to orgasm—at least, there *should* be. **Orgasm is a wild combination of electricity, oxygen, blood, hormones, muscles and motion from tip to toe**. At least, it *can* be. It is not simply a semen release, it is a body release—a flood of energy in motion. And there's always room for improvement.

We Haven't Talked a Lot About Orgasm

As you can tell, I have waited quite a while before talking to you about orgasm. And as you can guess, my choice has been very deliberate. The problem with talking about orgasm is that it tends to eclipse everything else. Start talking about "The Big O" and nobody wants to talk about "The Big A" (arousal), or "The Bigger A" (Attitude), or "The Giant L" (LOVE), or "The Boring P" (physiology), or "The Silent M" (masturbation). Nobody wants to talk about anything but orgasm!

Orgasm is a reward—it is the body's reward for giving it lots of attention and handling it with care. It is a reward that is given to those who take sex seriously—every aspect of sex. And the more you pay attention, the larger the reward.

For the past seven chapters, I have asked you to pay attention. I have asked you to learn new information, question old beliefs, notice subtle changes, experiment with new techniques. Instead of focusing exclusively on the brass "O" ring, you have spent seven chapters focusing on *all* of the elements that go into the finest recipe for making love to a man over 50. Now we *can* talk about orgasm. And his reward will also be your reward.

Starting with Breath

Breath fuels orgasm. See for yourself. The next time you are making love with your partner or masturbating by yourself, hold your breath as you approach orgasm and don't exhale until you have climaxed. Was it *half* as powerful? Was it strange and somewhat disappointing? Was it a total bust? That's because the strength of your breath gives your orgasm life. And it does the same thing for your partner.

Here's the problem—most men don't allow themselves to breathe powerfully through their orgasms. Remember that many men learned about orgasm in a climate of shame and secrecy, masturbating like quiet little mice under the bedcovers late at night or behind locked bathroom doors with potential intruders just feet away. Quiet little mice don't raise a ruckus with their breath—quiet little mice barely breathe, tiptoeing through their orgasms for fear of getting caught. Hence, the unremarkable sneeze-like sensation that so many men accept as orgasm.

In the following exercises, you're going to stir the mouse—stir him until he roars. You're going to teach him how to *really* sneeze. You're going to chase him till he's panting his way to an exciting climax, and hopefully a climax of your own. Don't set aside a special time or place for these exercises. Simply incorporate them into your regular lovemaking routine as you have the opportunity.

Synchronized Breath—The Technique

Recall one of the very first exercises you tried—the slow breath exercise from chapter 2. Like that exercise, it is very important for you to pay attention to *every breath* your partner takes when you are making love. Your goal this time, however, is to *gradually* magnify and intensify those sounds of his breath with your own, more forceful breathing. I emphasize the word gradually, because you don't want to make him self-conscious. On the contrary, you want him to feel more free.

He will take a breath, you will return that breath with a slightly fuller, louder, more forceful breath. He will take another breath, you will return that breath with a slightly fuller, louder, more forceful breath. Keep your mouth close to his skin so he can feel the difference, and close enough to his ear (if possible) that he can hear the difference. Think of yourself as a mirror reflecting back a more powerful, excited living image. Continue breath for breath, turning up the volume ever so slightly each time. Focus on his breath and *his* pleasure.

As your lovemaking intensifies, don't lose track of your partner's breath. It is very important that you are right there breathing more forcefully and more fully, but completely in sync with him breath by breath, as he approaches his climax. If you are fully in sync, the intensity of *your* breath will energize *his* climax.

In this exercise you are literally communicating through breath. You don't have to say, "Breathe more fully!" You don't have to say *anything*. Without words, the power of your breath is giving your partner permission to access the strength of his own breath. You're doing so much work in this exercise that you may not even notice your partner's shift, but as you breathe with greater intensity, your partner cannot resist following your lead. The shift is almost *automatic*. It's like entering a fast-paced conversation—your pace accelerates, too, even if it is not natural for you. You are energized by your surroundings.

Your partner's breath may not match the intensity of yours, but it will clearly be more forceful than usual. That force will increase with every change you initiate, and it will feed energy directly to his orgasm. Guess what? It will also feed energy into *your* orgasm. But perhaps you've already noticed that.

This is a very subtle technique that requires practice. And the initial results may be quite subtle as well. But the more you practice, the more powerful the result.

Breaking Sound Barriers

A lot of women know how energizing it is to flow with the sounds of their own pleasure: the *oohs* and *aahs*, the moans and groans, and the simple words like "Yes!" that paint such a complex picture of pleasure. It is my experience that the majority of men trail far behind their partners in the sound effects department. It is also my experience that men get more and more quiet as the years go by. Something about being *comfortable* seems to calm the male vocal cords. (That same comfort enables him to fall asleep in the middle of what you had hoped would be a romantic evening.)

But the release of sound, like the forceful release of breath, energizes sexual excitement and magnifies the experience of orgasm. And this becomes *increasingly* important with each passing year. As a man gets older, he needs to push beyond his comfortable sound barriers to enhance his experience of orgasm. And once again, his partner has the power to open that door.

Sounding Off—The Technique

During lovemaking, it is very important to be both a mirror and an amplifier for your partner's expression of sound. Don't wait until he is about to climax before you start. His very first sound is your cue to begin.

Every man will make *some* kind of sound when he is in the mood to make love when he is in the motions of making love and when he is in the throes of his own pleasure. He may give a bashful purr when you touch him, he may give an appreciative "hmmm" as he watches you undress. There will be subtle *ooh*s and *aah*s. He may even get very verbal. And, of course, there is always the sound of his breath. Your goal is to seize each of those sounds, however small and subtle, and return them to him with more heat, more force and more volume.

So here's how it works. Start with simple breath, as you did in the previous exercise. Follow him breath for breath, adding energy to each. If he makes little noises like "ooh" or "aah," return those same noises with increased intensity. If he gives a short "hmmmm," give a longer, louder "hmmmmmmmm." Don't be corny or silly. Keep your sounds sincere and very sexual. Stay with him word for word, sound for sound, breath for breath. As his excitement increases, increase the volume and force of every sound. Now watch as he rises to your level.

Boosting the sound factor like this adds energy and excitement at every stage of arousal, and pays off the most at climax, when maximum energy is released.

Muscles That Help, Muscles That Hinder
Muscle groups throughout the body play different roles in the experience of male orgasm. Various muscles spasm at the trigger point of orgasm, creating the waves of energy that move through the body. And the PC muscle, in concert with the urethral bulb, spasms to ejaculate a man's semen. In the world of muscles, that's all good news. The bad news is that many men try to "muscle" their way to a climax, keeping constant tension in their hips, thighs, buttocks and PC. As men get older and become less and less confident in the strength and predictability of their erections and orgasms, they try harder and harder to force the process with their various muscles. But this is actually the precise opposite of what gets the best results.

The path to orgasm is obstructed by excessive muscle tension. At arousal *peaks*, certain kinds of muscle tension can actually enhance the sensations of orgasm, but prior to those peaks, muscles get in the way. Tension in the legs and arms and buttocks and abdomen draws energy away from the groin, and exhausts muscles that could potentially enhance the full-body experience of climax if they weren't "frozen" or exhausted from the constant tension.

Muscle tension also draws *blood* away from the groin. We talked about this earlier in the book, but I want to talk a little more about it here. As men get older, they are increasingly vulnerable to what we technically refer to as *pelvic steal syndrome*. Pelvic steal syndrome is pretty much what it sounds like: a loss of blood from the penis into surrounding areas of the pelvis. Sometimes this blood is leaving the penis because the valves at the base of the penis have lost some of their efficiency. But more often, muscle tension is the culprit. Muscle tension in or around the pelvis steals blood from the penis, diminishing both erection and erotic sensitivity. Remember that muscle tension is supported by blood flow into the muscle tissue—that's the way muscles work. Tension in the thigh muscles, stomach muscles or buttock muscles has the potential to steal blood from the groin because of their proximity to that area. This doesn't mean you don't want your guy to have a great tight butt. It just means you don't want him to be clamping those pretty butt muscles while he's having sex with you!

PC muscle tension is the most curious culprit of all. When a man is squeezing his PC muscle, he feels as though he is drawing blood directly *into* his penis. Yet the reality is that PC tension is pulling blood *away* from the tissues that actually create his erection. And the more he squeezes his PC during arousal, the more he sabotages his own erection, his own arousal and his own orgasm.

Men give each other all kinds of advice about sex, but one thing they *never* tell each other is, "You have to relax those muscles!" You have to relax your thighs. You have to unclench your buttocks. You have to let that tummy out. And you have to release your death grip on that PC muscle. No one has ever told this to your partner. But you can tell him now, and the following exercise will help get the message across.

Body Feedback—The Technique

The best way to help your partner learn about the benefits of muscle relaxation is through the experience of a loving, erotic full body massage. In this massage, your goal is to slowly bring your partner to climax, using any comfortable combination of caressing and arousal techniques you are now familiar with. The most important thing is to keep your massage especially slow, letting your partner's arousal rise and fall again and again by alternating the area of focus. Don't spend *all* of your time massaging his penis—instead, move from the groin to other parts of his body, back to the groin, again to other parts of his body and so forth.

As your partner is enjoying the loving attention of his erotic massage, you want to pay careful attention to any signs of tension in critical muscles. Every time you feel tension in his muscles, let him know immediately by gently telling him, "Your thighs are very tense—you need to relax them," or "Your hips are very tense—you need to relax them," and so on. Keep giving him this "body feedback" until the tension dissipates. This may be difficult for him at first if he is used to clenching various parts of his body during sex.

Notice how his sensitivity to your touch is immediately enhanced as his muscles relax. Keep shifting the focus of your massage to delay his climax for at least twenty minutes, and keep checking on his various muscles. Give ongoing feedback. After fifteen or twenty minutes of massage, narrow the focus of your massage to his genitals exclusively and help him reach his orgasm. Ask him if he actually had a stronger climax by *not* muscling his way to orgasm.

◙   ◙   ◙

Your partner is not going to learn to relax every muscle in his body in one twenty-minute massage. Muscles take time to learn or unlearn behaviors.

Right now you are simply introducing him to something new, not asking for a miracle. But I encourage you to make this body massage a weekly event in your relationship for the next six months. It is *that* important. Let your partner reciprocate if that is something you would enjoy—there are probably many things he could still learn about *your* body, too.

Learning About PC Pleasure

Another very direct way to enhance a man's experience of orgasm is through stimulation of his PC muscle at the moment of climax. Though PC muscle tension *prior* to climax diminishes orgasm, PC stimulation *during* climax is a very different story. Remember that the PC muscle contracts during orgasm. Those contractions can be manipulated to intensify the experience. They can also be amplified to create a more forceful ejaculation. The first possibility is all in your hands; the second is dependent on your partner's willingness to prepare his body with a regular PC workout.

Touch the Muscle—The Technique

The best way to learn this technique is to practice during a sensual massage. A sensual massage that includes a lot of oral stimulation is best, because it brings your head and hands closer to the PC muscle, where you can see and feel what you are doing most clearly.

Begin with a slow, loving caress. Use your mouth to stimulate your partner's penis while using your hands to *delicately* massage his scrotum and explore the area behind it. Use your various caressing and massage techniques to raise his level of arousal and bring him closer to orgasm. Let the levels build gradually—this always adds to the intensity of the climax.

Ask your partner to let you know when he is about to ejaculate—he can cue you verbally or lightly squeeze your arm. As he gets closer to orgasm, be sure to have the fingers of one hand lightly resting on the folds of skin close to the PC muscle. *When he gives you your cue, take two of your fingers and press or push directly on the PC muscle.* This will send an exciting boost of energy through his body, momentarily electrifying his ejaculation. (NOTE: THIS PARTICULAR TECHNIQUE IS NOT RECOMMENDED FOR ANY MAN WITH PROSTATE TROUBLE.)

◨   ◨   ◨

If your partner has been diligently working his PC muscle (as presented in chapter 5), he has already experienced the difference a strong PC muscle makes during orgasm and ejaculation. His ejaculation has become more forceful, the volume of semen has probably increased and the PC contractions during orgasm are more focused, intense and pleasurable. This all happens automatically as the PC strengthens, and the confidence and sense of strength it engenders are often quite obvious. He may not be screaming at the top of his lungs yet, but he feels better, more powerful, more *sexual*, and that's difficult to hide.

Your partner can also learn to work his PC during his climax to add another level of power and pleasure to the experience. The secret is in learning when to squeeze the PC muscle and when *not* to squeeze the PC muscle.

Don't Squeeze . . . Squeeze—The Technique

It is best to practice this technique first during a sensual massage. As soon as your partner has enough confidence in his use of the technique, he can use it regularly during *all* lovemaking, including intercourse. Read through this exercise and explain to your partner beforehand, as the use of this technique requires some split-second timing.

Using your massage techniques and plenty of lubrication, help your partner work his way up the arousal ladder. With PC muscle control, he will have an easy time keeping the muscle relaxed during the various stages of his arousal. (The more he can keep *all* critical muscles relaxed—i.e., hips, thighs, buttocks—the easier it will be for him to climb the arousal ladder.)

PC amateurs tend to ride the PC muscle, but the older, wiser PC professionals have the power and wisdom to *let go*. As your partner gets closer and closer to orgasm, it becomes more and more critical that he keep the PC *relaxed. But the first natural spasm of his ejaculation is his cue to squeeze his PC muscle with full force.* This will both intensify the sensations of orgasm and add extraordinary force to his ejaculation. The trick is not to squeeze *before* the first reflex spasm. This can actually diminish his sensations and delay or even stop his ejaculation. He needs to wait for the first reflex spasm to hit, then magnify that spasm with his own PC control.

Come Early, Come Often

Men who are used to fighting their own urge to ejaculate will be quite stunned by the overwhelming sensations they can experience as they learn to manipulate their own ejaculation. But as a woman, you deserve to be stunned, too. And that's where the next exercise comes in.

Greased Lightning—The Technique

For this exercise, your partner should lie in bed face up, with you kneeling beside him. Begin with a lot of mutual foreplay and sensual massage. Be generous with the lubrication. Stay focused on the arousal process, allowing yourself to become more and more tuned in to the precise stages of your partner's excitement. Tell your partner that he needs to let you know when he is moments away from his own climax. When he gives you this cue, climb on top of him and let his penis penetrate you. Reach behind his testicles with one hand. When you feel the first spasm of his ejaculation, press on his PC muscle with two fingers. His ejaculation will hit *both of you* like a jolt of electricity.

It's in the Hips

When you go to a party, is your guy the king of the dance floor? Do people circle him to watch with awe and appreciation as he shows off moves and grooves that would startle Michael Jackson? Does he have an Elvis pelvis? Is he *the* Mambo King? Probably not. More likely, your partner is like most of the men his age: a little bit uptight when it comes to moving those hips. A man doesn't have to be a great dancer to be a great lover. You probably know that. But sexually speaking, **a tight pelvis is a punishing pelvis**—one that deprives a man of his own intense experience of orgasm. If you want to help your partner open himself to the power of his own climax, start by helping him open up his hips.

When you are having intercourse with your partner, what are you usually doing with your hands? Are they wrapped around his back, holding him close . . . are they holding his head so you can caress his face . . . are they grabbing the sheets and covers to keep you from sliding . . . are they turning the pages of that new novel you just bought? That's all fine (except the last one—unless it's a really *great* novel), but you can also be using your hands to help your partner loosen his pelvis and intensify his orgasm. You just have to know how.

- If you enjoy sucking on your partner's penis during foreplay, grab his pelvis with both hands as you suck on him, and rock him toward you so that his penis can go deeper into your mouth. Don't let his entire body rise off the bed—rock his pelvis at the joints so that only his hips are rising toward your mouth. This is a good starter exercise for introducing pelvic flexibility.

- If you are on top during intercourse, grab his hips with both hands and tilt them toward you rhythmically for deeper penetration. Be sure that your body weight is not keeping his hips pressed to the bed—support your weight with your knees, and stay as far forward as possible without losing contact with the penis.

- If he is on top of you during intercourse, grab his hips with both hands and work them to encourage loose-hip thrusting. In this position, you have the most strength and control to change the speed, direction and depth of his pelvic movements. Use the strength in your hands and arms to give him a real pelvic workout.

- Some men use their pelvis to support most of their body weight during intercourse—this immobilizes the area and diminishes the intensity of orgasm immeasurably. Your partner needs to learn to shift that weight to his knees or arms so that his pelvis is free to rotate. The most powerful climax position for a man on top is the position where his knees are supporting virtually *all* of his weight, so *all* major muscles can relax.

After these techniques have given your partner some experience rotating his hips back and forth, he will be ready for a more intense pelvic workout. The more his pelvis opens, the more his orgasm intensifies. Once he builds up comfort, flexibility and coordination, he may want to make this next exercise part of his daily grind.

A Pelvic Lambada—The Technique

To dance effectively pelvis-to-pelvis during intercourse, it is easier to have your partner as the one on top. This way, the bed will give *your* pelvis extra strength and support, which will be valuable once you begin your pelvic dance. What you want to do is slowly grind your hips (up and down, side to side), making it a challenge for him to keep his penis inside you. He will have to loosen his pelvis if he wants to avoid slipping out. After a while, vary your speed.

If your hips and his hips are pressed together, your partner will have an easier time following your lead—essentially, you are using your hips to train his hips. You *want* him to feel every movement of your hips so those movements can transfer to his hips. If you were on top during intercourse, he would not feel your movements in the same way.

Your hips are the best trainer. They are much stronger than your hands—particularly if they are being supported by the bed—so they can push your partner's hips around far more effectively. But let your hands assist, too—use them to grip his pelvis and help him move to your rhythm.

There Are No Victims in This Classroom

You have been working very hard to learn how to make your lovemaking more exciting, gratifying and memorable. With just a handful of exercises and techniques, a little education and a bit of attitude tweaking, you have already learned how to give your partner feelings of strength, vitality and pleasure that erase so many of the fears and concerns that creep into the bedroom when a man passes the age of 50. I know you are doing this not only because you love your partner, but also because it feels good to you, too. And why shouldn't it? I don't believe in bedroom martyrdom. You deserve every bit of pleasure that he deserves, and the excitement should always be mutual. But just to make sure you're getting your fair share, I've included one last exercise in this chapter with your needs uppermost in mind.

Remember how, in chapter 7, you used your partner's penis to stimulate yourself, as though it were a dildo? You are going to repeat that "masturbation" technique in this final exercise, but this time you are going to allow yourself to experience much higher levels of arousal and a well-deserved climax to remember.

The Perfect Moment—The Technique

Begin with your partner lying in bed face up, and you straddling his body with your legs. Try to keep the majority of your weight supported by your knees—remember, you don't want to cut off blood flow to his groin. Using plenty of lubrication, use your massage techniques and circulation enhancement techniques to slowly bring your partner's penis to attention. By now you should be very familiar with what he responds to most powerfully.

As his penis slowly swells, begin to use it like a dildo, massaging your vulva and stimulating your clitoris. Alternate your primary focus between his pleasure and yours to ensure that his penis remains somewhat erect. Experiment with your own levels of arousal. Let it ebb and flow. Use the assistance of your fingers to stimulate yourself, too, if that feels good. If you need your partner to rub your breasts, take his hands and show him. If you want him to insert one or two fingers in your vagina, take his fingers and guide him. Your pleasure is his focal point.

As you bring yourself closer and closer to orgasm, you'll need to pay more attention to keeping your partner's erection firm. Use *lots* of lubrication to facilitate this. When you know you are just moments from your own climax, let his penis penetrate you and thrust down on him as hard as you can. This time, the explosion is *yours*, though he may also climax from the intensity of your excitement.

Splashdown and Recovery

No conversation about orgasm and ejaculation would be complete without mention of something very interesting and surprising that happens to a lot of men as they pass the 50-year point in their lives. I'm talking about the flight from orgasm and ejaculation that I call "pleasurephobia."

As men get older, many become climax-shy. What was once a genuine source of pure pleasure is now a source of real conflict. They are intimidated by their own orgasms, and uncomfortable with their own ejaculations. Instead of being irrepressible between the sheets, they are hiding beneath the covers, genuinely reluctant to enjoy the sensations of their own release. What's going on here? The only way to understand this is to ask the men who are running. In the past fifteen years, I have done a lot of asking and a lot of listening, and what I have heard is something every woman needs to know.

Many of the older men I have worked with in my practice have explained to me that the fear of their own pleasure—their "pleasurephobia"—is something that has developed gradually over the years as they feel more and more drained from the experience of their own climax. "Orgasm and ejaculation put you out of commission," one man explained to me many years ago, "and the older you get, the longer it takes for the equipment to go back on line."

In chapter 3 we talked briefly about the male

refractory period—the rest-and-recovery phase of men's sexual excitement. For most men, the need for R & R increases over the years. Men who once felt fully recovered after twenty minutes may find that it now takes many hours. Some men claim it takes days. And it can't be forced. This is particularly unsettling for men who were once perfect performers. They don't like feeling debilitated by their own orgasms and ejaculations, and they don't like the feeling of powerlessness that they experience until the body has fully recharged.

During rest and recovery, some men can get an erection but are incapable of climaxing, some can actually climax but are incapable of experiencing an erection and some can't do anything but rest. As the time frame for R & R expands, men's discomfort grows. In the wake of these changes, it is understandable that many men lose their sexual playfulness and develop a "don't touch me" attitude. They lose faith in their body, they lose faith in their ability to consistently experience pleasure and they avoid intimate contact until that faith is restored.

Primitive Solutions for a Common Problem

There are many roads back from this place of reticence. But the only roads most men discover on their own are the roads marked "orgasm avoidance." If a man does not climax when he is making love, he is not going to lose his ability to have an erection—

certainly not for very long. Even an overworked penis *will* get tired eventually—orgasm or no orgasm—but recovery is relatively quick. Knowing this, some men will intentionally forsake their own orgasm and ejaculation. They won't let their body get to the brink, in order to worry less about the next erection. But guess what? This doesn't make them happy campers. Once in a while, as a sacrifice to the partner? Maybe. But on a regular basis? Forget about it. Men are used to having an orgasm and ejaculation when they make love, and the idea of *not* having an orgasm/ejaculation makes sex far less interesting.

Some men try to *minimize* the intensity of their own climax, gambling that a weak orgasm/ejaculation is easier for the body to recover from than a strong one. Perhaps this is a workable solution for some men—even if it is not a very pleasurable one. But more often, it is an inadequate solution. A climax is a climax. Even if it isn't a corker, the body may still need to go through all of the recycling motions and take its sweet time to recover. So what's a man to do?

Sophisticated Solutions for Sophisticated Lovers

To find other roads away from sexual reticence, a man needs to understand more about the physiology of his own rest and recovery process. Every man actually experiences two different levels of body recovery after orgasm and ejaculation. There is erection recovery—the finite period of time it takes before a man can experience another erection. And there is the recovery from orgasm and ejaculation—the finite period of time required before a man is capable of having his next orgasm and ejaculation.

Here's the critical piece of information: It is the ejaculation process specifically, not the orgasm in general, that initiates the more powerful down-for-the-count phase in a man's sexual cycle. It is also the ejaculation process that demands an increasingly lengthy recovery period as a man ages. In other words, **the body spends far more time recovering from its ejaculation than it does from its orgasm.** Perhaps you can now understand why women don't experience the same degree of post-orgasmic reticence.

Now here's some good news: Building up PC muscle strength seems to accelerate ejaculation recovery. So does a more frequent and consistent ejaculation schedule. And so does the introduction of a modest cardio-fitness regimen. Those are certainly several hopeful solutions for many men. But there is another: Men who have learned to climax without ejaculating—to literally suppress their ejaculation—have found an even more powerful way to resolve the "rest and recovery" dilemma.

Because ejaculation and orgasm are, physiologically speaking, two separate processes, a man can learn—through a series of exercises—to completely suppress his ejaculation without robbing himself of a powerful orgasm. He can even learn how to have multiple orgasms through this same suppression process! Ejaculation is important for prostate health, so this is not something a man over the age of 50 would want to practice habitually. But it certainly has its value.

If you are reading about it here for the very first time, the concept of ejaculation suppression may sound strange, or even impossible. I know how strange it sounded to me. Furthermore, learning this kind of ejaculation control takes a bit of work, and it is, admittedly, not for everyone. But I encourage every curious man to explore this possibility, and I encourage every woman to support her partner's exploration. It is a win-win path for every couple who takes the journey.

You can read more about ejaculation suppression and male multiple orgasm in my book *How to Make Love All Night*. Other good books have been written on this subject as well, and many useful articles have been published by popular magazines such as *Men's Health* and *Men's Fitness*. Go on line, or to a library or bookstore, and open your mind to new horizons.

Orgasm, Ejaculation and the Healthy Prostate

We all know that prostate problems are a concern for most men over 50. Because of the vulnerability of the prostate to enlargement and to cancer, the majority of medical doctors insist on annual prostate examinations after the age of 45, or even earlier. These exams—

though notorious for their discomfort and awkward-ness—are very important. But it is equally important that you and your partner pay regular attention to his prostate health.

One of the most effective ways for a man to keep his prostate in good shape is by clearing fluids from the prostate through ejaculation on a regular basis. This is not accomplished by taping an ejaculation schedule to your refrigerator next to the water-delivery schedule. It is accomplished by responding to the body's cycle of internal signals—the recurring urge to ejaculate. As a woman, you can't feel or see those signals. But you can support your partner's need to respond to those signals, even if this means encour-aging him to masturbate more frequently. Maintain-ing higher levels of arousal before ejaculation is also very effective because this engages the muscles around the prostate more actively. Now that you both know more about his arousal, try to make this your goal.

Two more components in a healthy prostate regi-men are PC muscle exercises and gentle external prostate massage. A strong PC powers the move-ment of fluid out of the prostate during ejaculation, discouraging weak ejaculation, fluid collection and its negative effects. A weekly prostate massage—using two fingers to lightly massage the area between the testicles and the anus where the PC mus-cle can be felt—is something I recommend for every man over 50. This can be done solo, or even better, as a pleasurable partner exercise. The important thing is to start doing it now.

PLEASE NOTE: Prostate problems, circulation problems, diabetes and other disease processes will always interfere with sexual functioning and sexual pleasure. Regular medical check-ups, a healthy diet and a physician-approved cardio-fitness program are your greatest allies in the lifelong campaign for comprehensive sexual health.

9

Your *Body*, Your *Changes*

I could have easily devoted every chapter of this book to some important aspect of your partner's body and your partner's changes. But even if I went into exhaustive detail worthy of a Ph.D. dissertation, I wouldn't be giving you the complete picture. Yes, men can go through many sexual changes as they move through the second half of their lives. But *so do women*. And **many of *your* sexual changes—whether they are emotional or physiological, temporary or permanent—can have great bearing on *his* sexuality.** Sex is a couples issue. Every fear affects two people. Every mood swing affects two people. Every piece of new information affects two people. Every change—positive or negative, his or yours—affects two people.

Sometimes a woman can be a mirror for the man in her life, highlighting the reality that we cannot stay young forever. Other times, a woman's sexual intensity and power can be a discouraging reminder that men tend to lose their potency more quickly. What is your body telling your partner? What is your level of sexual drive (or lack thereof) telling your partner? What is the intensity of your erotic desire telling your partner? And how is this affecting his interest, his enthusiasm and his ability to perform? Does your sexuality silently support your partner, or does it silently scare him to death? All of these issues will be examined in this chapter.

Male sexuality is not the only sexuality that is surrounded by myths and misunderstandings, and I will also use this chapter to explore some of the popular myths about women, sex and aging. We need to talk about body image and its effect on desire. We need to talk about orgasmic potential and orgasmic realities. We need to talk about estrogen therapy, testosterone supplements and the real facts about menopause. Then you need some "anti-aging" exercises of your own—simple techniques that consistently yield miraculous results.

A Brief History of Time

What will getting older mean to you? Are you sitting right now in your sexual prime, excited about your prospects for the future? Or are you already wrestling with the possibilities or realities of female menopause and its consequences?

One hundred years ago, menopause wasn't making front-page headlines. Many women weren't even living long enough to worry about something so "trivial." Then came psychoanalytic thinking, and menopause suddenly became important. The end of a woman's fertility window became a subject of great debate, and concerned analysts worried about the massive psychological impact of this "change of life." The men worried from a safe professional distance, in the comfortable corridors of their analytic offices, and women silently worried at home.

Before the 1960s and women's liberation, women who went through menopause typically experienced a classic shift: They gained weight, they grew more facial hair, they watched their features grow coarse, they lost their sex drive and they lost contact with their femininity. Sex lost its urgency. Sex became less of a priority. And for many, sex simply ended.

Women's liberation finally brought menopause out of the closet. It became okay to admit you were having symptoms of menopause—even to brag about your symptoms! Hot flashes became acceptable dinner table conversation. Much of the shame and confusion evaporated. Yet the change in the status of menopause had a peculiar twist: To celebrated writers such as Germaine Greer, menopause and the aging process were freeing because they lifted the burden of male sexual oppression. You were now free because you didn't have to worry about *him.* Clearly, many steps were taken in the right direction, but a few steps were still heading down negative roads that emphasized separateness, not partnership.

In the 1980s, menopause became a medical problem that—like all medical problems—would certainly be resolved with medical solutions. On the plus side, it was clearly recognized that a hysterectomy and/or removal of the ovaries and/or menopause itself were creating hormonal changes that had the potential to affect the sex drive, to affect body tissue and to affect women's overall health. On the down side, the answer was a blanket prescription of estrogen replacement therapy (ERT). Like every blanket prescription, some women got exactly what they needed, and many more did not. Women were feeling more hopeful, but not necessarily more sexual.

Finally, the more sensitive, more female-empowered 1990s arrived. Both doctors and patients began to recognize and appreciate the unique hormonal profile of every woman, be that woman premenopausal, menopausal or postmenopausal. More complex therapies were developed, often using combinations of estrogen, progesterone and testosterone. For some women, these new medical solutions are miraculous. For some, they are adequate. And for some, they seem scary—with the 1990s sensitivity came a respect for the body that encouraged caution, not experimentation.

And now we head into the new millennium. What

face will the future of menopause have, and will that affect sexual relationships after the age of 50?

You Are Not Your Mother's Menopause

As we march boldly into the next century, it is clear that we need an equally bold new view of female menopause. Menopause does not mean the end of sex. But could it be a new *beginning*?

Contrary to popular belief, there is very little research on specific changes in sexual *pleasure* that are triggered by the onset of female menopause. There is no hard evidence that women enjoy being touched any less, or held any less, or caressed any less, or fondled any less, or stimulated to orgasm any less. There is no evidence that women have fewer orgasms. There is no evidence that it takes any longer to reach an orgasm. And there is no evidence that an orgasm is any less pleasurable.

Here's what we *do* know: As women age and go through menopause, our skin and hair usually change, typically becoming more dry. There is usually some thinning of the vaginal walls. There may be dryness of the vaginal walls (though there are topical creams and also simple exercises that can alleviate that dryness). If we are not taking estrogen, our periods will ultimately stop, but there may be many months or even years of unpredictability. Moods can be more unpredictable, and desire may, at times, wane. This doesn't all happen like a bolt of lightning.

It is not an *event*, it is a process that unfolds over—
typically—several years. And yes, there are some challenges. But it is certainly not the death of sex.

**Prevailing sexual attitudes have a profound effect
on sexual reality.** And if you are bracing for the worst,
you have a much better chance of finding the worst.
Think about the attitudes we used to have about men-
struation. Young girls were told they would have
cramps and be sick, so they had cramps and were
sick. Think about the attitudes we used to have about
losing one's virginity. We were told it would be
painful, and it was. Now think about what you have
already been told about menopause, and how you are
bracing for the worst. The time for change is now.
You can, on the one hand, dutifully re-create your
mother's menopause or your grandmother's menopause. Or you can rise above that history and take
charge of your changes. You can cave in to stereotypes and fear, or you can chart a new course. I opt
for the latter, and I am hoping you will join me.

What Are You Telling Your Partner About Your Own Fears of Aging?

Attitudes about aging are rarely something we manage to keep to ourselves. Maybe we don't come right
out and say it, but somehow—through our body language, our sexual reticence, our sexual disinterest, our
staring in the mirror, our change in clothing style, our
obsession with hair and makeup, our envy of others—

the message is getting across. Truth is, many of us *do* come right out and say it! We ask our partners, "Do you love me?" "Do you still find me attractive?" "Do you think I'm sexy?" "Why are you still with me?" "Would you like it if I got breast implants?" "Do you think I'd look better if I had a facelift?" "Do you think *that* woman is pretty? Do you think *that* woman is sexy?" "Should I get liposuction?"

For some women, that's *subtle.* These women can be far more negative and discouraging with comments such as, "I hate my body!" "Don't look at my cellulite—it's gross!" "Every woman here is prettier than I am." "I'm fat, fat, fat!" "Wouldn't you like to sleep with *her*?" "I don't know what you see in me."

Let's face it: Most women don't wait for menopause to start airing their fears and insecurities. If you are afraid of becoming less attractive to your partner, you have already let him know. If you are afraid of losing your sexual vitality, you have already let him know. If you are afraid of being replaced by a young, sexy thing half your age, you have already let him know. And your need for positive reinforcement and loving assurance can feel constant, creating an exhausting responsibility for the man you love.

What so many women fail to understand is that the men in their lives value the loving connection they have built through the years with their partners more than they could ever value a new pair of breasts. As one 69-year-old male client told me, "My wife is incredibly sexy. Sure, I can appreciate the beauty of another woman. But that's where it stops—with appreciation. My wife is the woman I know and love, and her body is the body I know and love."

When a man loves his partner, there is a richness that can only develop through years of connection. If you have created this richness, your partner sees a vital, sexy woman every time he looks at you. He's not comparing you to every pair of legs that walks down the street. He's not comparing you to what he sees in a magazine or on TV. He's not comparing you to *anything*, unless you are driving him to comparison by endlessly pushing these issues into his face. **Don't make your fears his fears**—this is the biggest mistake a woman can make.

What Is the Change in Your Sex Drive Telling Your Partner?

Under the absolute best of conditions, your sex drive will necessarily fluctuate over the course of your lifetime. This is true for you, and it is true for your partner. Hormonal changes, stress, diet, exercise, illness and the clock keep us very busy adjusting and readjusting to our sexual self-experience. This is normal. Most of the changes are temporary, particularly the ones that are driven by hormones. Often, the worst changes are temporary. But the changes come. Count on it.

So the question is, do you beat yourself up about

this, blame your partner for this or just accept this as part of life?

The changes in your sex drive are telling your partner that you are going through physiological changes. Your partner will understand this if you allow him that opportunity.

- These changes are *not* saying, "I don't love you."
- These changes are *not* saying, "I'll never be horny again."
- These changes are *not* saying, "I'm interested in another man."
- These changes are *not* saying, "I don't want you to be nice to me, appreciate me, communicate with me or touch me."

Don't let your confusion over the shifts within you become his confusion. If there's one message *you* need to hear, it's the message that says, "You may need some tests to check on the hormone levels in your body because hormonal supplements may be in order for you."

What Is the Change in Your *Desire* Telling Your Partner?

There is drive, and then there is desire. While drive has its roots in basic physiology, desire has more complex origins. Anger, love, stress, fear, hormones, fantasy, lust, time, a change in the weather, a new pair of panties—these are some of the elements that create desire.

Desire is a very strange and wonderful beast. But the one thing you can count on is that desire will ebb and flow. Yes, you may feel white-white-hot every single day of a torrid one-year affair, but in a stable relationship, desire will not remain a constant forever.

As your desire changes, you may worry that these changes are sending negative messages to your partner. "Does he think I've lost interest?" "Does he think he's lost his touch?" So many women have been conditioned to believe that part of their role in a partnership is to be the embodiment of desire. Men are drawn to women filled with desire—at least, that's the way the stories often go. But does your partner *really* expect you to be the passionate, excited woman he dated years ago? Does he want you to get a little wet every time he looks at you? Unlikely. Remember, your guy is wrestling with his own changes. His desire is far from constant. Some days it's nonexistent, and those days sometimes turn into weeks or even months. He may appreciate the fact that you can empathize.

The issue, once again, is not seizing upon your various changes and blowing them up into monstrous problems. If you let your own aging process grind you down and depress you, you're far more likely to drag your partner down in the process. If you let your own aging process anger you and fill your head with critical voices, your partner will feel powerless and confused. If you have an endless litany of negative self-judgments, your partner is going to *assume* you're judging him the very same way. **You have to learn to live with a new you, and to love that new you—a you that is changing every single day.** If you are open and self-accepting, your partner will also feel acceptance. Instead of being afraid or defensive, he will be supportive. Then, together, you can start to figure out ways to reinvigorate the system.

Turning Back the Clock

When it comes to fighting the effects of her own aging process, a woman's best defense is a good offense. Don't sit around waiting for the time in your life when you are feeling sexless and hopeless. It doesn't matter if you are 35 or 55, the time to start that good offense is *now*. Today. This very moment. And it starts with a daily regimen of age erasers.

Let's start with something very simple: lubrication. Not the kind you buy in a bottle, but the natural kind that your body offers you every day. One source of natural lubrication that is usually overlooked is the fluid that is released by the Bartholin's glands. These glands, which are located under the skin of the outer vaginal lips, right around the middle of the vagina, secrete small amounts of a thin fluid that is part of your lubrication system. This is not the fluid you are most familiar with—the fluid that is secreted through the walls of the vagina—but it is part of your body's natural vaginal maintenance.

Fluid from the Bartholin's glands keeps the outer tissues of your vagina more soft and supple. It is the fluid that supports your message of "welcome." Stimulating these glands increases their fluid production and secretion. So let's begin our slow transformation here, then work our way in.

The Bartholin's Technique

You will need to remove all of your clothing for this exercise (at least from the waist down). The exercise begins with a slow genital self-caress. This is something best done lying comfortably in bed. Begin your self-caress by softly stroking sensitive areas of the body such as your breasts, stomach and thighs. Slowly move your caress to the vaginal area. Your goal is not to excite yourself or masturbate, only to lovingly caress. Using your index finger and middle finger, slowly caress the outer lips of your vagina. Now press lightly on the Bartholin's glands and feel the gentle secretion. You probably won't be able to see the Bartholin's glands precisely because the openings are very small and buried in the tissue, so finding the right spot may require a little bit of trial and error. But this is not very complicated. Start at the midpoint of the outer lips and move slightly up or down from there. When you feel the secretion, you will know that you have found the approximate location.

Continue your genital caress for five to ten minutes, pressing on the Bartholin's glands every thirty seconds. Do not press too hard or rub too roughly—these glands respond to very gentle pressing. Try to repeat this exercise on a daily basis, just as you would put on hand cream on a daily basis.

It's Not the Heat, It's the Humidity

While the Bartholin's glands contribute to the lubrication of surface vaginal tissues, the majority of our vaginal lubrication—particularly internal lubrication of the vaginal walls—occurs when blood flows into the groin. As blood flows into the genital area, it fills the tiny blood vessels in the vaginal walls. This swelling pushes our natural lubricating fluids out through these walls in a process that is called *vaginal sweating*. If there's fire in your loins, there's plenty of precipitation. When your blood is boiling, your natural fluids runneth over. As a woman, you have probably known this instinctively all your life—it's that always-gorgeous experience of "getting really wet." Now you know the physiology.

So it turns out that your partner is not the only one who depends on blood circulation to keep his system up and running. **The key to your vaginal health, and natural lubrication, is healthy blood circulation.** And there is something you can do about it right now, because any form of massage or genital caress that activates and intensifies circulation in the groin will keep your vaginal tissues more consistently well lubricated and healthy. This is the simplest, most effective way to stave off the process of vaginal thinning and drying.

Earlier in this book you learned how to actively move blood into your partner's groin area—to literally push it—when you were focusing on his needs for enhanced circulation. It was the "spokes of the wheel" technique. Now it's time to focus on the spokes of *your* wheel.

The Technique

You will need to remove all of your clothing for this exercise, and to lie comfortably on your back. I recommend taking the time to do an intense full body-caress, starting with peripheral areas such as the hands and feet, followed by the arms and calves and then the abdomen and thighs. Your goal throughout the exercise is to move blood into the genitals, so your stroking shouldn't be constantly changing directions up and down the body. Movement should be in only one direction: toward the groin.

Start slowly. One hand. The other hand. One foot. The other foot. One arm. The other arm. One leg. The other leg. And so on, and so on. Imagine there are arrows painted all over your body pointing in the direction of your groin. Follow those arrows. Stay focused on your goal, and allow yourself to feel your vagina naturally lubricating itself as blood moves into the groin. Unlike some other caress techniques, it is appropriate here to have a firmer hand. A more vigorous stroke will reach deeper into the tissues and muscles, moving more blood and generating more lubrication.

Orgasm is not your goal in this exercise (though there will probably be times when you can't resist the temptation). Stay focused on activating your circulation and allow yourself at least twenty minutes of this delightful lubrication technique. While it is important to practice this at least once a week, women with current concerns about vaginal dryness should make this part of their daily health regimen. Even practicing this technique for five or ten minutes a day will make a significant difference in the health and suppleness of your vaginal tissues.

Soft, Softer, Softest

While I am a big believer in letting the body do the jobs it does best, there is also nothing wrong with supplementing these two age eraser techniques with massages that utilize other forms of lubrication.

I encourage women to approach this as though they were having a wine tasting. Buy a variety of lubricants—water-based, oil-based, even prescription estrogen cream—as long as they are clearly indicated to be safe for vaginal application. Incorporate these lubricants into your full-body massage, one by one. You could try them all in one session, or try a different product each day for several days. How does each one feel during the application process? Do the positive effects linger? For how long—minutes? hours? days? Evaluate the results and consider integrating your favorite(s) into your daily lubrication regimen. And remember, **when you are fighting the war against aging, there is no such thing as too much lubrication!**

Room for Two

While the Bartholin's gland massage is a delicate technique that is best done alone, the circulation-enhancing massages (with or without the addition of supplementary lubricants) are ideal exercises to invite your partner's participation. By now, your partner should understand the importance of enhanced blood circulation and lubrication, having experienced both firsthand in the techniques you have already generously introduced him to. His desire to help you feel more youthful, more sensual and more sexually motivated is likely to make him an eager volunteer. Furthermore, as you have already discovered, these are also very sensual experiences for the "masseur."

As long as it is clearly established ahead of time that these are non-demand techniques that are not a necessary prelude to sex, your partner may be thrilled to have a regular opportunity to make such an intimate, pressure-free physical connection. Don't let your own reticence or awkwardness deprive both of you of this opportunity. This is a place for growth.

Too Tight to Tango?

As the years of our relationships pass, our sexual attitudes and experiences are efficiently stored in our minds, and in our bodies. For women, one of the most crucial storage bins in the body is the pelvis. If we feel free and open and encouraged through our history of sexual experiences with our partner, we feel that freedom in the pelvis. But if we have been left feeling frustrated, disappointed, discouraged or angry too many times, we often lose that freedom.

If you are going to open yourself to many more years of relationship growth and more expressive lovemaking, you're going to need a body that is cooperative. While many changes come from the inside, through emotional understanding, self-acceptance and healing, important changes can also work their way in from the outside. And a good place to start is at ground zero—the pelvic region. If you want to be sexy, you *must* feel sexy. And you can't feel sexy with a tight pelvis.

Men will always tell you that they know how a woman makes love from the way she moves on the dance floor. I hate supporting any sexual stereotypes . . . but I think the guys are right on this one. I tell every woman who comes to my office that every day you age is a day that you should be *dancing*. Opening the hips through the pleasure of dance will fight against sexual lethargy, habits and routines. It will fight the forces of fear and other negativity. And it will fight the clock. If you keep shaking it, you will never lose your desire to be making it. I'm trying to be funny, but I'm feeling quite serious. And I'll prove it to you with the following exercise.

Pelvic Rhythms—The Technique

It is important to do this exercise alone until you have practiced for a very long time. Your partner's presence has the potential to make you feel self-conscious and locked down. It is best to wear very loose clothing.

Start by playing some of your favorite dance music. If you like your music loud, pump up the volume so that the music completely surrounds and embraces you.

Close your eyes, and for the first few minutes, let yourself simply *feel* the music. Don't move your feet and run away from it. Keep your feet planted and let the music penetrate. After a few minutes, allow the music to move fully into your pelvis, and allow your pelvis to respond. What you want to do next, for at least ten minutes, is rock your pelvis *from front to back* without moving any other parts of your body. Imagine that you are supporting a hula hoop in time to the music. It's probably been a while, but I know you remember. This may sound silly, but it may help at first to use a real hula hoop to help your body remember the exact motion.

Let those hips rock and roll, and feel the muscles loosen. Don't sway, don't jiggle and don't shimmy. Slower is better, especially at first. Frantic movements are not helpful. The important thing is to give your hips a long, luxurious workout of sexy, liquid pelvic rolls. In ten minutes you will probably feel sexier than you have in ten years. You are loosening muscles, ridding yourself of sexual prohibitions and inhibitions *and* invigorating the pelvis with blood. It's a potent combo. Imagine what you would feel like if you did this every day.

After you have completed at least ten minutes of rolls, you can continue with a few minutes of free dance. But don't start to move those legs until you've really worked the pelvis hard.

Waking the Body with a Loving Squeeze

Earlier in this book we spent a lot of time talking about the importance of your partner's PC muscle. I am wondering if all of this talk got you thinking about your own PC muscle. Did you try a flex or two of your own? Did you think about practicing *his* exercises? Truth is, your partner is not the only one who has much to gain from a strong, healthy PC. Toning your PC muscle on a daily basis makes arousal, penetration and orgasm more powerful because such strengthening tightens the vagina and builds muscle mass. Consider some of the things that a fit PC can do for *you*:

- Increased PC muscle mass heightens the sensations of arousal as blood rushes to the groin in response to stimulation.

- PC muscle strength creates more intense orgasms as blood rushes *out* of the PC during the muscle spasms of orgasm. With a larger, stronger muscle, much more blood collects in the muscle tissue, hence, a greater exit rush.

- PC muscle strength helps you tighten the vagina— something particularly desirable for women who feel stretched from multiple childbirths (or just from many years of penetration).

- PC muscle strength will give you greater capacity for being multi-orgasmic because it allows you to maintain higher levels of arousal.

- PC muscle strength will enable you to get more of a "grip" on your partner's penis—that will stop him from dozing off!

- PC muscle strength is the best defense against incontinence—another concern that comes with the years.

- Increased PC muscle mass draws more blood to the groin on a daily basis—sex or no sex—keeping the vagina healthier.

That is a lot for just one muscle, and a compelling argument for starting your own PC workout. But there's more. I think that the most important reason for a woman of *any* age to build a strong PC muscle and keep it strong for the rest of her life is this: **A daily regimen of PC muscle-building is a daily regimen of intense sexual awakening.**

Bringing your energy, your blood and, most important of all, your *focus* to the groin awakens your sexuality, invigorates your sexuality and sharpens your experience of your sexual self. So many women hide from their own sexuality. They narrow the window into their own erotic potential and get accustomed to feeling a mere fraction of their own sexual strength. The reasons for this vary, but the result is the same: sexual powerlessness. PC strength is the perfect solution to this all-too-common problem. Focusing on the PC forces you to acknowledge that strength, filling you with a sense of sexual power. It's like turning back the hands of the clock.

Working It Out, PC-Style

Maybe you have already discovered the power of your own PC muscle. Maybe you have a daily regimen of Kegel exercises (basic PC exercises that were first developed by the obstetrician Dr. A. H. Kegel) that you perform faithfully. I hope you do. But it is more likely that you will be doing these exercises for the very first time. That's not a problem—I have taught these exercises to women in their eighties! So let me start by reminding you that the PC muscle is actually a group of muscles that runs from the pubic bone in the front of your body to the tailbone in your rear. Like your partner, it is the muscle you use to stop the flow of urination, and that is how most women become acquainted with the muscle for the first time. Take a few minutes to get reacquainted with the muscle. After that, you're ready for the workout.

PC Discovery for Women—The Technique

Locate your PC muscle by placing your index finger or middle finger about one inch (to the first knuckle) into your vagina. Internally you will feel a sensation of pulling inward or upward.

With your finger inside you, squeeze as if you were trying to stop the flow of urination. The muscle that tightens around your finger is the PC. Keep your stomach muscles, thigh muscles and buttocks muscles relaxed to avoid PC confusion. Now squeeze the PC again. The muscle may not feel very strong right now—it may barely feel like a muscle at all. But that will change very quickly once you start your regular workout.

If you are having trouble isolating the PC muscle, and perhaps feeling a bit confused, the first thing you need to do is relax. Take a few slow, deep breaths. Now experiment with *other* muscles close to the groin. Tighten your stomach muscles, then release and relax. Tighten your thigh muscles, then release and relax. Tighten your buttock muscles, then release and relax. Get to know the feelings of these separate muscles, and the sensation of complete relaxation. Now try once again to squeeze the muscle that stops the flow of urination. Was it clearer this time? Could you feel it close around your finger? Continue your rotation between different muscle groups until you are confident you have isolated the PC.

PC Basics for Women—The Technique

Once you know where the PC muscle is and what it feels like to tighten it, you are ready for your PC program. For one week, do a simple series of squeezing and releasing—fifteen repetitions, twice a day, every day. If you need the help of your finger inserted in your vagina to keep you on track, that's fine. You won't need this forever.

After one week, try to start holding your PC squeeze for a count of two full seconds before you release. Squeeze, hold for two seconds, release. Repeat this ten times twice a day for another week.

Your third week, increase your workout to twenty repetitions (squeeze, hold, release) twice a day. Maintaining your workout at this level will bring you the basic PC strength you need. If you find yourself craving more, refer to the other PC exercises found in chapter 5.

Back in Circulation

You can't talk about making love without talking about healthy circulation. You need it to activate *your* sexuality, and your partner needs it to activate *his* sexuality. Through many chapters we have focused on blood circulation in the groin, and I know you have learned a lot. But we also need to talk about the larger picture—the full-body circulation picture. Sometimes feeding the fires of love calls for fantasy and imagination, but it is my experience as a health professional that these fires are fed most effectively by caring for every single inch of the body with a circulation-enhancing diet and a regular regimen of basic exercise.

With no exercise and a poor diet, the fire goes out. It's that simple. **A woman who doesn't exercise and doesn't attend to what she puts into her body is saying to her partner, "I don't care."** On the other hand, a woman who treats her body like a precious gift and lavishes it with a program of regular exercise and wisely chosen foods is saying to her partner, "I want to be strong, I want to be sexy, I am still interested in sexual pleasure and I'm willing to work to get it." That is a very powerful message.

Exercise and effective circulation go hand in hand. It's the primary reason why *everyone* feels sexier when they have activated the body through reasonable exercise. What kind of exercise is reasonable for you? That depends, of course, on your age, your lifestyle and your interests. But you have so many options: walking, dancing, yoga, swimming, stretching. All simple, all basic, yet all make a difference. This doesn't have to be complicated to be effective, and it doesn't have to be expensive. It just has to be part of your day. And if it is something you and your partner can share—a ritual that gives you an extra opportunity for connection—that's even better. Do it for your relationship, do it for your heart or do it for your groin—just make sure you do it!

Now let's talk about food. When you look at your diet, think again about circulation. What kinds of foods and other substances do you welcome into your body? Are these things that promote circulation? Coffee, sugar, alcohol, cigarettes—are these substances sex-busters in your relationship? Think about this carefully. Think about this, too: A lot of women are discovering subtle food allergies that create a chronic sense of lethargy. Could this be happening to you? Every day more and more research reveals how, for example, wheat allergies have a direct impact on blood circulation. High-carbohydrate diets are also under fire from many health professionals. How many times in the past year have you found yourself saying, "Not tonight, I'm too tired"? Sure, it could be stress, or it could be all that hard work you do every single day. But maybe, just maybe, your diet is doing you in.

When you were 25 years old, you probably were able to get away with just about anything. Junk food, junk living, no exercise, it didn't matter. But none of us is 25 anymore. And the older you get, the more you will feel the symptoms triggered by bad choices and body neglect. Yes, your partner needs to deal with these issues. But this is also the time to reevaluate *you*. It's wonderful that you are so concerned about your partner, but you have to mind your own store! Don't wait for a big problem. Start before the fires go out. And set an example that will be an inspiration to both of you.

Hormones *Can* Help

I am not the greatest proponent of "better living through chemistry"—I always look for more natural solutions to potential problems, and I have tried to share many of those solutions with you here. So I'm not going to spend a lot of time talking about your hormones. But I am going to ask you to pay serious attention to their impact on your self-image, the changes in your sexuality and the overall picture of your health. Let's face it, our hormones keep us busy. **We are, as women, all vulnerable to the strange cycles and complex changes the body creates from within.**

You probably know the range of symptoms of a radical shift in body hormones: thinning hair, thinning skin, unavoidable weight gain, dryness and/or cracking of the skin, loss of bone mass, erratic menstrual cycle (or termination of the cycle), complex mood changes and so on. There are many hormones at work here, and that makes for a lot of potential changes. But hormonal activity is not the mystery it once was, and hormonal supplements may be surprisingly helpful to counter some of these changes. *Some women do need hormonal supplements*. This doesn't have to be dangerous, and it doesn't make you any less a woman.

A competent physician can help you evaluate your hormonal profile and stop you from becoming a victim of your own internal chemistry. Doctors finally understand that every single woman has a unique profile, and requires a unique approach. Your profile is affected by your current age, the age you reached puberty, your medical history, your medication history, your childbirth history (number of children, spacing of children), the specifics of your menstrual cycle, your birth control methods and so on and so forth. It's complicated. And that's why I believe that *every* woman over the age of 40 should have her hormone levels evaluated. Good information makes smart choices possible.

Birth Control Backlash

Have you ever used birth control pills? If your answer is yes, I want to give you some extra encouragement to have your hormone levels evaluated *now*. When you first started taking birth control pills, there's a good chance that your libido was *energized*. Part of this energy certainly came from feeling the burden of pregnancy fears being lifted; but another part of this energy is a typical by-product of a pill-induced testosterone boost. As years pass, however, something very different can happen: The pill may start to actually *deenergize* the libido.

When the libido starts to wane, most women assume that they are just getting older and naturally slowing down. But it may be birth control chemistry that is slowing you down. A hormonal evaluation will help you sort this out, and give you options to counter these changes.

Taking Responsibility for Your Body and Your Changes

Hormone talk makes a lot of women want to bury their heads in the sand. They abhor the feeling of turning their bodies into chemistry experiments, and I know that feeling all too well. Yet running and hiding is not the answer—not if you want to be making love to your partner way into the new millennium.

It's time to take responsibility for your body and your changes. There are more answers and better answers out there for women than ever before. Some of these answers are in books that offer straight talk on hormonal supplements. Some of these answers can be found in support groups. And some of these answers can be found in other information sources such as the World Wide Web. As Internet resources go, my personal favorite is powersurge.com, an on-line site devoted entirely to menopause and its consequences. Check it out. There is much to learn. And much for your partner to learn, too!

10

Heart to Heart

We've talked about him and we've talked about you. We've talked about anatomy and we've talked about technique. We've talked about attitudes and we've talked about myths. We've talked about arousal and we've talked about orgasm. We've even talked a little about diet and exercise. Now it's time to talk about *love*.

Your sexual future with your partner will be influenced by so many factors, but the most crucial factor of all as the years pass will be the quality of your romantic relationship. Love and sex may be two very different things, but the power of love to make or break a sexual relationship over time is truly formidable. It's formidable at the age of 50. And at the age of 60. And at the age of 90. And this book wouldn't be complete without a chapter dedicated solely to the heart.

When a sexual relationship is young and strong, it can do wonders for the relationship as a whole, yet also mask a multitude of sins. Great sex makes a couple feel connected. Great sex makes a couple feel compatible. Great sex makes a couple feel as if they are communicating. And great sex makes a couple feel in love. Sex is an extraordinary glue, a glue that can keep even a marginal relationship feeling vital and valuable. But what happens when that glue starts to lose its strength? What happens when it takes a little more hard work to make sex work? What happens when the power of Father Time takes its toll on our chemistry, our energy and our fragile bodies? This is when the relationship is tested.

It takes a solid *romantic* relationship to keep a *sexual* relationship solid year after year. It takes a loving relationship, and a very *committed* relationship. When a sexual relationship stops being problem-free, too many couples discover that they have not been doing hard work as a couple. They have been letting sex do the work, and without that perfect magic to count on, the relationship can get very confused.

As a sex therapist, I often find that I am spending far more time talking with my clients about relationship issues than I am talking with them about sex. That shouldn't really come as much of a surprise, but it is certainly a surprise to them. Most couples arrive at my office certain that they are in need of a simple mechanical tweaking. But they leave with a very different understanding—that's my job.

In this chapter, I need to complete my job for *you*. **Great sex, at *any* age, does not begin in your bed. It begins in your heart.** Hormones may be flowing freely, and all vital body parts may be in working order, but if the emotional pipelines in your relationship are getting clogged with gunk, making love to a man over 50 is going to become more and more problematic. So let's spend some time now with my favorite organ—the muscle of love that rarely skips a beat. We need to ensure that every chamber is open and always ready to welcome the one you love.

A Loving Workout for a Loving Heart

Do you give your partner a loving hug the first moment you see him every morning? When you are reunited after a long day of separation, do you give him a sweet kiss? *Everyone* says, "I know my partner loves me." My question is, what are you doing every day to make *sure* he knows? The heart does not run on empty for thousands and thousands of miles. Your partner may "know" that you love him, and you may know that *he* loves you, but the knowing is only part of the recipe for lifelong connection. The heart needs to *feel* that connection—physically feel it—on a regular basis to stay open and completely assured.

You probably know through years of experience that one sure path to your partner's heart is through loving words. Perhaps another path is through your mutual passion for art, theater, music, film or food. Maybe your hearts get activated by spending time together on a quiet afternoon. Or maybe your hearts melt every time you look at pictures of your children. These are all essential paths. Yet the direct physical path to the heart is equally powerful, and one that few couples ever discover. When you physically engage the heart, you engage it emotionally as well. It may be a different approach than the one you are used to, but the results are surprisingly powerful.

While you may not worry that there is plenty of love in your partner's heart, you probably *do* worry about his heart's strength and health. Perhaps your partner has already had a few medical challenges, or maybe he has had serious struggles. When our partner is over 50 we worry about "pushing" his heart, and this tends to make us shy away from intense sex. What we never let ourselves imagine is that we can help strengthen and even heal his heart through loving, sensual pathways. You just have to be courageous and make the heart connection.

Feeling the Beat of a Loving Heart

Few of us are at a loss for words when we talk about things that come straight from the heart. But our words are always ever so slightly abstract. Making the heart connection begins by going from the abstract to the concrete. And the only way to do that is to feel the beat—the actual pulsating, round-the-clock beat that is filling the body with life. Let's begin with a few simple exercises that your typical couple would never even think of. Once you try them, you'll think of them constantly.

Nurturing Hearts—The Technique

While this is a nonsexual exercise, it is best done without either partner wearing clothing. Start by asking your partner to lie down comfortably on the bed. Lie down next to him, on your side, draping your free arm across his body and relaxing your head on his chest *directly* over his heart (the left side of his chest). Be very still, very quiet, and listen for the beat of his heart. Try to feel *his* heartbeat. Feel how it slows down as he grows more comfortable with you resting in this lovely, intimate way. After at least five minutes of listening and enjoying, take your partner's hand and press it to *your* heart. Give him a chance to physically connect to your beat as you remain connected to his. Give yourselves ten minutes in this position. When you have completed the exercise, make your disconnection slowly and gently—**an abrupt disconnection is never easy for the heart.**

Synchronizing Hearts—The Technique

Are you ready to snuggle up close? For this exercise, you and your partner need to lie together on your sides, both facing the same direction, pressed up close to each other. Let your partner take the front position first—this means that the front of your naked body should be pressed fully to the back of his naked body. Curl up slightly so that both of you are in a "spoon" position. Now reach around to the front with one of your hands and press it to his stomach.

Start to pay attention to his breath—you can feel its rhythm with your hand on his stomach—with the goal of synchronizing your breath with his. Take three very long, slow breaths. If your partner is breathing rapidly, encourage him to take slower breaths, like yours—give him another clear example if necessary. Take your time breathing in sync until you can feel a matching rhythm. Now slowly shift your focus to his heart. Move your hand from his stomach to his heart. If your other hand is free, reach around and place that on his heart as well.

Feel the beat of his heart slow down as he relaxes into your breath. Imagine that your hands are saying to him, "This is my heart, too." Can you feel your own heart keeping rhythm with his? Immerse yourself in that rhythm. Allow yourself at least ten or fifteen minutes to enjoy this connection. Once again, disengage slowly and gently when you have finished.

◘　◘　◘

I always used to think "two hearts that beat as one" was a more interesting premise for a science fiction film than for a sex aid. But I have learned the soft way—the soft, loving way—that fundamentals of physiology can open the doors to dreamy fantasy.

Synchronized breath and synchronized heartbeat are very sophisticated ways to synchronize your lovemaking. When two people who love each other feel so thoroughly connected, there is often a seamless transition into loving sex. This may not be your standard foreplay, but it is a gorgeous alternative when you're in a more spiritual mood.

Reaching Out, Reaching In

I love to get women excited about the prospects of making a more genuinely loving connection with their partners. I love to give advice, share powerful exercises and support the process of genuine healing. When I am giving one of my pep talks to women, you will often hear me say this: **If you want a more loving reality, don't wait for it . . . create it.**

Women wait. They are used to waiting for what they want. We've heard too many stories about damsels in distress waiting to be rescued from their towers, and heroic women waiting for their men to return from the war. Even if your relationship has lasted dozens of years, you may still feel frustrated by your lack of access to your partner's heart. You may still be waiting.

If there is one thing I have learned in my practice, watching the men who come into my office for help, it's that most of these men don't wait. When they want something—something they know they need— they ask for it. Or they take it, even if that includes a magazine in the waiting room!

As women searching for growth, we need to embrace the male model. Sometimes this is about turning your life around—going back to school, taking a new job, moving to a new town—even if it is truly terrifying. But sometimes it's about turning your *love* around by making a different connection with the heart. If you want access to your partner's heart, sometimes you just have to reach in with your own heart and grab it. You have to take control. You have to create change. Consider these next three exercises as examples.

All Smiles, All Heart

A smile opens the heart. It's so simple and so true. You know what your partner's smile does for your heart. But if you are like most loving women, you are probably prepared to wait weeks or even months to see that smile. From this day forward, the waiting is over. . . .

A Loving Mirror—The Technique

The next time you are making love to your partner, pause for a moment to look at his face. Touch it with your hands, then hold his face in your hands—your faces should only be twelve to eighteen inches apart. Look into his eyes. Now smile at him—not a small, tight, fearful smile, but an open, loving smile that he can clearly see. Notice how he will mirror you, and smile right back. It's a reflex he can't control, but the smile is real, and it will touch both of your hearts.

A Perfect Smile—The Technique

Once again, pause for a moment during your love-making and look carefully at your partner's face. Touch it with your hands, then hold his face in your hands—your faces should be less than two feet apart. Look into his eyes. As you hold his gaze, slowly start to massage his chin and his jaw—do this with the intention of relaxing his facial muscles. After a few minutes of gentle massage, after you've felt his muscles relax, move your hands to his mouth and run your fingers along his lips. Now gently mold his lips into a smile. Create his beautiful smile with your hands as though you were a sculptor molding it from clay. As he releases tension and control and relaxes into this smile, note your own smile forming. Feel the gentle heart connection that has been established. As you break the gaze and let him go, do so slowly and gently.

◧ ◧ ◧

As you first introduce these techniques to your partner, it is most effective to practice them during lovemaking when you have his rapt attention. But once your partner becomes comfortable with these heart-warming gestures, try to practice them more regularly. For example, practice them when you first look at each other in the morning or when you are about to separate for a few hours or when you greet each other at the end of the day or when you are having a quiet evening moment watching television or reading. In other words, don't think of sex as your only opportunity to make this special heart connection. As I said, don't wait . . . create!

Emotional Surveillance, Emotional Connection

People who are truly in love look into each other's eyes much more often than two friends, two acquaintances or couples who are only casually connected. Behavioral scientists have studied this phenomenon for years, and the results are always quite striking. The question is, what are we looking *for*? And the answer is not a simple one.

Sometimes we are searching for love, and sometimes we are searching for a mirror—for a source of reassurance and validation. Sometimes we are looking for signs of anxiety or distress (a friend of mine calls this "emotional surveillance"), and sometimes we are doing it for pure pleasure. Once in a while, we are staring at a loose eyelash and wondering what to do about it.

But now try to imagine something different. Imagine making a conscious decision to take the next ten minutes to stare into your partner's eyes. This is a bonding exercise that is not as simple as it sounds. It may make you self-conscious; it may make you want to giggle. But done with great seriousness, it produces serious connection. Try it soon. Do it holding your partner's hands to your heart, or pressing your hands to his heart. This is another simple technique that sends old emotional walls tumbling down.

Working the Muscle of Love

The last few exercises are not for the faint of heart. You will need to disrobe, and you will need to be vulnerable. These are romantic exercises with strong sexual undertones *and* overtones. They are different styles of making love, with *four* participants in the room. Yes, I said four. Four participants. Four entities. But don't pass out yet—I'm not trying to sell you on experimental group sex. I'm talking about you, your partner, and your two loving hearts. One plus one plus two. That's four. Call it the new math.

The most exciting lovemaking you will ever experience is the lovemaking that takes place in the presence of two vibrant hearts. Your hearts must be awake and aware of each other, which means that *you* must be awake and aware. Though we have good intentions, most of us can let our hearts rest quietly during sex. We know the heart connection is there, but we don't take the time to really check in. We don't go searching with a flashlight. We don't pay attention to each beat. These final exercises will remedy that problem and give you the thing you crave most: a thriving bond of the hearts.

Caressing the Heart—The Technique

This exercise is similar to the genital caress you learned in chapter 7. But this time you will need one free hand to reach out to your partner's heart. Practice your sensual caresses, loving touches and exciting massage techniques. Use plenty of lubrication, and experiment with his levels of arousal. But always have one hand resting lovingly on your partner's chest, right at the place of his heart. The message you are sending is simple and sincere: "When I am with your body, I am with your heart."

For a variation, practice your caresses and massage techniques with your head resting on his chest, one ear listening to his heartbeat. Or press your lips softly against the larger veins of your partner's neck where you can feel his pulse every moment.

When you have focused on your partner's pleasure for twenty or thirty minutes, give him the chance to focus on yours. Let him give you a loving genital caress with *his* head resting on your heart, his head pressed against your chest or his lips softly pressed to the strong veins in your neck. Or perhaps you would prefer to let him be a loving witness to your genital *self*-caress. Do your own self-massage, but welcome him into it by bringing his hand to your chest, his lips to your neck or his head to your chest. Mmmmmm.

Making Love to the Heart—The Technique

Sexual intercourse is the ultimate act of love and vulnerability when doors to the heart stay open. The next time you make love to your partner, make a conscious effort to walk through those doors by following these simple instructions.

Speaking practically, this last heart exercise is most effective with you on top and your partner underneath. You need to be in control of the thrusting to ensure that enough attention is being given to both hearts. With practice, you will be able to switch positions and experience the technique from both exciting perspectives.

The exercise begins as your normal lovemaking would begin. Once your partner is inside you, create a slow, even rhythm. Now make your physical contact with his heart. Depending on your size and "fit," it will be easier to either rest your head on his chest (directly over his heart), press your lips to the large veins in his neck, or rest one hand softly on his chest. Don't exert a lot of pressure—this is not a cardiac massage—just make the soft heart connection.

After a time of slow, even thrusting, vary your speed to intensify arousal. Feel how the heart responds. Your partner's erection may not be completely consistent—if he is tuning in to your heart, that may be the place of his greatest consistency. Don't make hardness an issue, and don't let it interrupt the heart connection. Just stay pressed together until his erection recovers.

Continue to experiment with this loving connection. Slow down to a still point. Speed up to a thrill point. Give yourself permission to let time slip away. Turn off distracting voices that come from your active mind, and give yourself over to the pure emotional experience of feeding the open heart.

Every Decade Is a Sexual Adventure

Perhaps there is no greater experience of intimacy than this—your partner inside you, and your hearts inside each other. And that is where I think we should end our love lessons.

I promised you a book about possibility. I promised to give you insight, to give you ideas, to give you reassurance, to give you a new perspective and to give you practical techniques that are easy to share. My problem is that I could keep on writing and writing. That is what happens when you truly believe in love.

How do you make love to a man over 50? I guess you now know that you have so many options. Making love to a man over 50 is an ongoing exercise in relationship growth. Growth that continues at 60, and 70, and 80, and . . . With every year, you will feel more, you will care more, you will love more. Of course there will be days when you're just too tired, and nights when you'd rather watch TV. There will be weeks when you're too preoccupied, and sometimes months when you're just out of sync. But if you take good care of the fundamental bond, your love will bring you back to that place of connection where bodies press against each other and excitement is stirred. Never give up on that place of connection. It is a place your partner is counting on and dreaming of. It is a place where time stands still.

Simple Solutions for Physical Problems

In the beginning of this book I talked about the myth of male impotence, and the clumsy and insensitive use of this very terrifying label. But, as a practicing sex therapist, I must also acknowledge that there is a small percentage of men who do indeed suffer from true organic impotence. And this percentage increases with age.

In addition to organic impotence, there are a number of other medical complications that affect men's ability to function sexually, and a small but significant percentage of the over-50 male population also struggles with these challenges. But this should not mean that sex for these men, and for the men who are truly impotent, is to be written off as a lost cause. Many of these men already have found ways to have very rewarding sexual relationships with their partners.

And many more who have the desire just need to find the right path.

Most of the observations I make as a sex therapist in clinical practice must be kept in the strictest confidence. But after almost twenty years of work in this field, there is one observation I never hesitate to share: A man's sex life is not over unless he *wants* it to be over. While all of the exercises and techniques I have presented in this book may not be entirely appropriate for men with organic impotence or other medical complications, there is a different set of viable options for these men. In this section I will discuss these many options, and offer my professional opinion on the various avenues you and your partner may ultimately consider.

Before your partner chooses to pursue any solution—medical or otherwise—to the limitations in his sexual functioning, he needs to sit down and talk with you. Sometimes the only thing that is missing in your sexual relationship is a way for your partner to express his sexuality without feeling pressured, awkward or inadequate.

Sex is a couples issue. The two of you need to talk about your choices, and you need to talk about your needs. Many men go through great distress and great expense to make changes that their partner does not need or want. Many men agonize over changes in their sexual functioning that their partner does not care about or even notice. I do not want something like this to happen between you and your partner. This is no place for surprises, miscommunication or misunderstandings. **A problem is not a problem unless it is making someone unhappy**. And medical solutions are not always the best solutions.

The Right Solution Requires the Right Diagnosis

No man should have to accept the label of "impotence" without a clear and verifiable diagnosis by a trained professional. The problem is that your general practitioner may not be that person. I would discourage any man from accepting a diagnosis that does not come from an experienced urologist who *specializes* in impotence. This diagnosis is even more reliable if it has confirmation from an experienced psychotherapist; never underestimate the power of your partner's emotional makeup. Yes, it will cost a few extra dollars to go this very comprehensive route, but in the long run, you will be saving more than just money.

How is impotence diagnosed? Some people attach the label if a man can't get an erection while having sex with his partner. Yet this same man may be able to masturbate when he is alone, having both an erection and an orgasm. Clearly, this is not impotence. If your partner falls into this category, his struggle to perform in your presence is due to either the mechanics of your lovemaking or the emotional complications of your lovemaking. Clearly, something is not working. But that doesn't make impotence the correct diagnosis.

When your partner has two different sexual realities—one with you, and one without you—this is material for a therapist and/or sex therapist to help you explore.

The Nocturnal Test and Its Limitations

Many doctors use the Nocturnal Penile Tumescence test (NPT) to evaluate a man's sexual functioning. In this test, doctors use a machine called a Rigiscan that attaches directly to the penis, electronically measuring the activity of the penis throughout the night. The Rigiscan can be used for one night, but it is more valid if it is used several nights in a row. If a man does not have morning (waking) erections or periodic nighttime erections during his sleep cycle, most doctors interpret this as a clear sign of organic impotence. But this is simply not true.

For starters, this machine has its limitations. The machine often malfunctions, and the gauge often detaches partially or falls off completely. As you might imagine, it isn't easy sleeping with a machine hooked up to the penis. A woman can make a much better diagnosis of her partner's nighttime erection activity by simply monitoring it herself. Pick a night when your partner can go to bed early and you can stay up for several hours and watch his body.

There are other limitations to the NPT, including a number of temporary conditions that can interfere with the process of nighttime and morning erections.

Depression is one of those conditions. Stress is another. And adding the label of impotence to the emotional pile is only going to make these other conditions worse.

Certain sleep disturbances also interfere with the erection process. Nighttime erections in healthy men occur during REM (rapid-eye movement) sleep, also known as Emergent Stage 1 sleep. But if a man is chronically deprived of REM sleep because, for example, he suffers from sleep apnea, he may not be spending enough time in REM sleep to have these erections. In addition, the sleep deprivation will also impair daytime functioning—the penis does not work well in the absence of restful sleep. It's a vicious cycle that is easily misdiagnosed as impotence.

Various prescription medications also interfere with the nighttime *and* daytime erection process. These medications will "fail" your partner on his NPT test, but the diagnosis of impotence would be inappropriate. Once again, it is an experienced urologist who can help you sort this out. **Maybe all your partner needs is a change in some medication to a more erection-friendly alternative, or a change in the dosage of some medication.** Always look for simple solutions first.

Taking a Closer Look

If a urologist cannot find a simple explanation for your partner's performance issues, he/she will probably want to take a closer look at your partner's anatomy and physiology to get valuable information.

A blood test is one simple and useful diagnostic tool. Some older men experience a large drop in testosterone levels that would show up in the blood work. These low levels can be enhanced with a testosterone skin patch that is placed on the scrotum. This simple remedy is quite popular, but it is effective only if there is a true testosterone deficiency. The patch will not override other physiological complications.

If it is not a simple testosterone issue, some type of sonogram or MRI may be recommended. One useful test is called *dynamic cavernosography*. A dye is injected into the penis or into an artery in the leg or abdomen (ouch!), and then followed as it moves through the penis. The urologist can see if all of the tissue chambers of the penis are capable of filling, and leaky valves can also be spotted. This information will help the urologist determine the best choices for a long-term treatment plan.

Making Smart Choices

If your partner has been diagnosed with organic impotence and it is a diagnosis you both trust, you will need to make some choices. Viagra is certainly one option, but it is not your only option. In the pages that follow I have briefly outlined the *many* choices you both have, starting with the least expensive choices and the choices with minimal side effects. I encourage people to always look for the easiest, least expensive options with the fewest potential side effects. That makes sense, doesn't it? It takes a little longer to work your way through the alternatives, but the payoff justifies the effort.

Sex Therapy

There is always a chance that a medical diagnosis is not accurate and that simple exercises will produce results. These exercises can't make the problem worse. At the very least, the couples exercises will bring you and your partner closer together. Start with the exercises you can find in the many reputable books on the market. Also consider learning some of these exercises under the guidance of a sex therapist. A sex therapist is trained to notice *small* details in your approach to lovemaking that can create *big* problems. Try a few sessions—eight sessions is more than enough to experience *some* result. Once again, the exercises a therapist will teach you can't make things any worse. And they will help you and your partner learn to communicate better about what you each *really* want from your lovemaking.

Over-the-Counter Assistance

Many people report that certain over-the-counter erection products work. I'm sure this is true for some percentage of the population, and it's certainly an avenue that is worth exploring before you consider the more heavy-duty prescription medicine route.

Popular enhancement products include ginseng, yohimbé and DHEA supplements. **But do note that some of these products cannot be taken by men with heart problems, including irregular heart rate or rapid heart rate. Always ask your physician *first*.**

Prescription Medicines

There is a very good reason why millions of prescriptions have been written for Viagra since it was first introduced—for many men struggling with organic impotence, the pill works. Taken approximately one hour before sex, Viagra clearly changes a man's response to stimulation of the penis. What it does, essentially, is relax the smooth muscle at the base of the penis and allow blood to flow in. The penis must still be stimulated—it is not a magic wand—but direct stimulation does produce a strong response in an impressive percentage of the men who take the drug.

Earlier in this book I talked extensively about the potential limitations of prescription medicines; now I need to talk about the potential positives: **There is definitely a future in performance-enhancing medicines.** Many "penis pills" are in development right now; there will probably be something new next month, and a dozen more choices next year. That's fine, as long as serious caution is exercised. Manufacturers are required to label their warnings and contraindications carefully, but it is your job to *read* those labels and take them seriously.

The two pills you are likely to see next are phento-lamine and apomorphine. Phentolamine is a drug that is already being used in injection form, but the oral version is on its way. It is a vasodilator that works by drawing blood into the tiny blood vessels in the erectile tissue of the penis. Apomorphine is a very different kind of drug that supposedly works on dopamine levels in the brain at the "erection center." This drug is likely to affect desire as well as performance.

It will be interesting to watch what happens as these drugs become available and men start lining up to get their prescriptions filled.

Penile Suppositories

Some men are more comfortable with a medical solution that is highly localized—one that focuses exclusively on the groin and doesn't have the potential to affect the entire body. The penile suppository is one good example of a localized treatment option. The suppository—a very small pellet—is actually inserted into the tip of the urethra. Then the penis is slowly stroked or massaged for about ten minutes to give the pellet the chance to dissolve and work its way into the tissues of the penis to produce an erection. Strange? For some. But many men are happy with the results.

Vacuum Erection Device

Vacuum pumps cannot, as some advertisements promise, permanently enlarge the penis. These pumps *can*, however, facilitate the erection process, assuming the devices are used properly. Here is how the pump works: A plastic cylinder fits over the penis and air is pumped out of the cylinder with an attached hand pump, creating a vacuum. Creating this vacuum causes the penis to inflate with blood. The man then places a ring around the base of his erect penis to hold the blood in—this ring can be kept on for up to twenty minutes. It's a labor-intensive process, but it can work. What is important is the careful placement of the ring; placed incorrectly, it can cause bruising or bleeding, and injure the veins in the penis.

Penile Injection

The penile injection is another very effective (albeit off-putting, for many), highly localized medical solution. The man actually injects the chemical papaverine or prostaglandin (trade name Caverject) directly into his penis ten minutes before he is ready to make love. Though this is not for the faint of heart—and potentially damaging to erectile tissue if used in excess—the results are quite impressive when the instructions are carefully followed. Frequent (daily) use of this particular method is also discouraged because of the potential build-up of scar tissue at the injection site.

Penile Implants

I recommend penile implants only as a last resort. This is not because they don't work—they can work very well—it is because they usually necessitate very complex surgical procedures that are expensive and often painful. And they are usually permanent. In this ever-changing world of medicine, permanent choices can lead to regrets down the road.

There are actually several different kinds of implants. There is the simple penile implant—semi-rigid silicone rods are inserted between the cylinders of natural tissue in a man's penis. What bothers some men about this is that they have a permanent erection, and the bulge is not easy to conceal. There is also a more flexible implant made of silicone with a wire core. This implant can be bent up to create an erection, or bent down.

The implant that most closely mimics the erection process is also the most elaborate and potentially problematic. A tube is surgically implanted in the penis, a reservoir of fluid is inserted in the fatty tissue of the abdomen and a little pump mechanism is implanted under the skin of the scrotum. When a man desires an erection, he squeezes the pump, filling the tubes with fluid from the reservoir. After sex, he presses a release valve attached to the pump and the fluid returns to the reservoir, "deflating" the erection. A finite percentage of these units break down, which is not surprising considering the complex nature of the device.

Of course, new types of implants are being manufactured all the time, and the implant option is an option worth exploring with a urologist. But my personal recommendation is that a man explore all of his *other* options thoroughly before choosing an invasive—and generally permanent—surgical procedure.

Stay in Touch

I feel very positive about many of these treatment approaches—I have many clients who have experienced impressive results. But I also need to point out that in my experience, the majority of these devices and substances (implants aside) do not always perform *consistently* over time. Very few work well *all* of the time. So it is important to have a backup plan, and to keep an open mind to solutions that will appear in the years to come.

I also need to restate the obvious because the obvious gets lost when you start investigating the various impotence remedies: An erection does not necessarily make for good lovemaking. There is *no* substitute—not a mechanical one and not a pharmacological one—for sexual awareness, sexual communication and sexual consideration. A clumsy, inconsiderate, selfish or indifferent lover is not suddenly a prince because he has an erection.

Finally, I want to emphasize that a diagnosis of organic impotence is not carved in stone. I encourage every man, regardless of his plan of attack, to practice the morning groin massage (chapter 5) every single day, and have a regular weekly routine of genital caressing exercises (chapter 7) with his partner. Men need to stay in close touch with their bodies, and we all need to stay in close touch with our partners.

Recommended Reading

Brecher, Edward. *Love, Sex, and Aging—A Consumers Union Report*. Mount Vernon, NY: Consumers Union, 1984.

Davis, Elizabeth. *Women, Sex & Desire*. Alameda, CA: Hunter House, 1995.

Diamond, Jed. *Male Menopause*. Naperville, IL: Sourcebooks, 1997.

Keesling, Barbara. *How to Make Love All Night*. New York: HarperCollins, 1994.

———. *Sexual Healing*. Alameda, CA: Hunter House, 1996.

Kingma, Daphne Rose. *The Men We Never Knew*. Berkeley, CA: Conari Press, 1994.

Ojeda, Linda. *Menopause Without Medicine*. Alameda, CA: Hunter House, 1990.

Penney, Alexandra. *How to Make Love to a Man*. New York: Dell Publishing Co., 1981.

Reichman, Judith. *I'm Not in the Mood*. New York: William Morrow, 1998.

Sheehy, Gail. *Passages: Predictable Crises of Adult Life*. New York: E. P. Dutton, 1976.

———. *Menopause: The Silent Passage*. New York: Random House, 1995.

———. *New Passages: Mapping Your Life Across Time*. New York: Random House, 1995.

———. *Understanding Men's Passages*. New York: Random House, 1998.

Vliet, Elizabeth Lee. *Screaming to Be Heard— Hormonal Connections Women Suspect and Doctors Ignore*. New York: M. Evans, 1995.

Zilbergeld, Bernie. *The New Male Sexuality*. New York: Bantam Books, 1992.

Index